CREATIVE
Craft Lettering
Made Easy

Marie Browning

NORTH LIGHT BOOKS
CINCINNATI, OHIO
www.artistsnetwork.com

Creative Craft Lettering Made Easy. Copyright © 2005 by Marie Browning. Manufactured in China. All rights reserved. The patterns and drawings in this book are for the personal use of the reader. By permission of the author and publisher, they may be either hand-traced or photocopied to make single copies, but under no circumstances may they be resold or republished. No other part of this book may be reproduced in any form or by any electronic or mechanical means including information storage and retrieval systems without permission in writing from the publisher, except by a reviewer who may quote brief passages in a review. Published by North Light Books, an imprint of F&W Publications, Inc., 4700 East Galbraith Road, Cincinnati, Ohio, 45236. (800) 289-0963. First Edition.

Other fine North Light Books are available from your local bookstore, art supply store or direct from the publisher.

09   08   07   06   05   5   4   3   2   1

Library of Congress Cataloging-in-Publication Data

89009000374682

Browning, Marie.
  Creative craft lettering made easy / Marie Browning.-- 1st ed.
     p. cm.
  Includes index.
  ISBN 1-58180-647-7 (alk. paper)
    1. Handicraft. 2. Lettering. I. Title.

TT157.B78495 2005
  745.5--dc22

Editor: Jennifer Fellinger
Designer: Marissa Bowers
Layout Artist: Jessica Schultz
Production Coordinator: Robin Richie
Photographer: Christine Polomsky, Tim Grondin and Al Parrish
Photo Stylist: Nora Martini

fw
F+W PUBLICATIONS, INC.

Metric Conversion Chart

TO CONVERT	TO	MULTIPLY BY
Inches	Centimeters	2.54
Centimeters	Inches	0.4
Feet	Centimeters	30.5
Centimeters	Feet	0.03
Yards	Meters	0.9
Meters	Yards	1.1
Sq. Inches	Sq. Centimeters	6.45
Sq. Centimeters	Sq. Inches	0.16
Sq. Feet	Sq. Meters	0.09
Sq. Meters	Sq. Feet	10.8
Sq. Yards	Sq. Meters	0.8
Sq. Meters	Sq. Yards	1.2
Pounds	Kilograms	0.45
Kilograms	Pounds	2.2
Ounces	Grams	28.4
Grams	Ounces	0.04

About the Author

A rich family tradition of craftsmanship nurtured Marie Browning from an early age. Always drawn to jobs and education that included fine arts, crafting and creating, Marie knew her passion for creativity would someday become her business. This vision became a reality as new opportunities opened the door to the launching of *Marie Browning Creates*, a design and consulting business in the craft trade.

Marie's crafting ability is driven by her fine arts training and love of traditional crafting disciplines. Calligraphy, soapmaking, fragrance crafting, papermaking, parchment crafting, stenciling and découpage have all come to life in her hands. She has written more than fourteen titles in the creative-living field, including books on soapmaking, paper crafts, garden crafts, packaging and simple bookbinding. Her writing career has also included numerous magazine articles, project sheets for manufacturers and project instructions for Web sites.

Active in product development within the craft industry, Marie has assisted Environmental Technology Inc. with several programs, including *AromaGel*, an innovative and award-winning gelled air freshener, *EasyCast* and *Tile Art*. Marie also helped develop and design Fiskars's recent *Parchamoré* parchment crafting system.

Marie lives and runs her business on Vancouver Island in beautiful British Columbia, Canada. Her first love is her family: husband Scott and three children, Katelyn, Lena and Jonathan. Find out more about Marie at www.mariebrowning.com.

Acknowledgments

It takes an exceptional team working together to produce a quality publication. My heartfelt thanks go to those who helped me with their encouragement and exceptional talents. They include my editor, Jennifer Fellinger, photographer, Christine Polomsky, and the whole F+W publication team, who made me feel so welcome during the photo session in Cincinnati.

To all the manufacturers that generously supported the projects in this book with quality products and technical assistance, and to my assistant, Gloria Davenport, a million thanks.

Being surrounded by a supportive family also makes doing projects like this possible. Special thanks and love to my children and to my husband, Scott.

Table of Contents

Projects 26

Introduction

It is increasingly popular to use quotes, inspiring words and letter designs in home décor. There is nothing new, however, about the human impulse to decorate one's surroundings with marks that tell a story. Prehistoric cavemen recorded events with pictures on cave walls, Egyptians painted their temples with hiero-glyphics, and medieval royalty adorned their castles with floor-to-ceiling tapestries. Today, we feel the same desire to incorporate mark-making and lettering into our living space. By using decorative lettering in our own creative ways, we become a part of this history.

People often associate "lettering" with "calligraphy." The word *calligraphy* comes from the Greek *kalli*, meaning *beautiful*, and *graphia*, meaning *writing*. But if the thought of calligraphy scares you, and you consider your handwriting anything but beautiful, don't worry—this book is still for you! The most important thing to remember is that you do not have to be a calligrapher to use lettering for beautiful home décor projects. In fact, you don't even need to like your own penmanship. Designed for crafters of all abilities, this book shows that there is a lettering style and technique for everyone!

> The most important thing to remember is that you do not have to be a calligrapher to use lettering for beautiful home décor projects.

Over the course of two thousand years, the basic western Latin alphabet has developed into a wide range of decorative alphabet styles, from simple block printing to elaborate scripts. Hand lettering is still a basic technique, but today's technology has made it easy to create remarkable letters in many font styles. Hand lettering and computer-generated lettering represent two ends of the lettering spectrum; there are lots more fun, creative and easy techniques to learn, many of which I've included in the following pages.

No matter which technique is your favorite, I think you'll find the projects exciting and inspirational. The manner in which letters are laid out on a surface is an expression of creativity, and the emotional power you can convey goes far beyond the meaning of the words themselves. And, when you do the lettering yourself, you'll discover what a great source of pride and achievement these projects can be.

Lettering Terms to Know

Throughout the projects in this book, I'll be using various terms to describe different aspects of lettering. Even if you are already familiar with many of these terms, you may find this illustrated list a helpful resource. As the illustrations show, a simple change in case, size or spacing can often dramatically affect the look of lettering. Try experimenting with the variables listed below to see how you can alter your lettered projects.

AB CD

| **Uppercase** | refers to capital letters, also called *majuscules*, which in Latin refers to the height of the letters.

ab cd

| **Lowercase** | refers to small letters, also called *minuscules*.

craft

| **Freestanding lettering** | refers to printed lettering when the letters—each standing alone—are not joined.

| **Cursive** | refers to joined lettering, such as handwritten script.

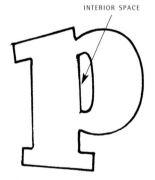

INTERIOR SPACE

| **Interior spaces** | occur in letters that have closed sections, as in the letter *P*, shown above. These pose extra challenges when cutting or using stencils for lettering. See the *Stenciling* section on pages 16–18 for tips on how to deal with interior spaces.

BRIDGE

BRIDGE

| **Bridges** | are the sections within each letter or number stencil that hold the design together and reinforce the stencil. Bridges block out the surface as paint or ink is being applied, leaving parts of the letter unpainted.

R R

laugh

| Flourishes | are decorative finishing details added to letters. When adding decorations to letters, you should still be able to read the word. In the example above, the letter *R* on the right is still legible, but it has been enhanced with a *swash*, or an extension of a stroke.

| Bouncing the letters | is a way of positioning letters so that they do not all sit on a common line. Be careful when you apply this technique, as too much bounce can make the word(s) difficult to read. In the example above, the style and arrangement of letters convey a fun and relaxed feeling, perfect for the word *laugh*.

time began in a garden

RAINBOW

| Letter size | refers to the height and width of each letter, which can vary from letter to letter or word to word—or not at all—to create different effects in your craft projects. In the example above, *garden* is lettered larger to emphasize the importance of the word and to add variety to the composition.

| Letter spacing | refers to the spacing between characters in a word. The *mechanical spacing* of old-fashioned typewriters allotted the same amount of linear space to each character whether it was narrow or wide; the resulting letter combinations were often visually inconsistent, appearing either too crowded or too far apart. Today, computer-generated text yields more visually consistent results. When lettering something yourself, take into account the visual perception of spacing. *Optical spacing* allows a designer to adjust the spacing between characters at will to achieve the desired effect. In this example of the word *rainbow*, the narrow letter *i* might have contrasted to the wide letter *w* had the spacing not been adjusted for a more natural and balanced look.

Basic Lettering Techniques

There are many ways to create lettering for your craft projects. With the wide variety of tools and materials currently available, the possibilities seem almost endless. In the following pages, you'll see several different lettering techniques that can be used to give your projects a unique touch.

USING A COMPUTER TO GENERATE LETTERING

Today, with so many readily accessible computer programs and high-quality color printers, it is easier than ever to create beautiful lettering. Equipped with just a few basic computer skills, you can lay out lettering in a document, then print it on your choice of paper. The lettering can be incorporated into your project as a design element or as a pattern. Because different computer programs require different steps for laying out text, this section does not include step-by-step instructions. However, it does offer a few simple ideas for computer-generated lettering, taken from the projects in this book. It also presents an explanation of the basic variables involved in computer-generated lettering.

| **Print on your choice of paper** |

Many kinds of paper can be used in an ink-jet printer, including vellum, card-weight paper, some handmade papers and text-weight colored and decorative papers. Here, I've selected some favorite sayings to fit the project theme, then printed them on a piece of decorative paper. Always run a test print on the back of the decorative paper to make sure it prints successfully.

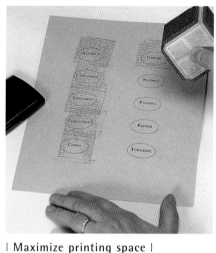

| **Maximize printing space** |

"Gang-up" the computer-generated text on your paper by fitting as many words or letters on one page as possible, maximizing the use of the paper. Above, words are printed on lilac card stock, framed with an oval outline and decorated with rubber stamping. The outline will serve as a guide for trimming the words quickly and uniformly.

| **Print, then treat surface** |

Print out letters and words on plain paper, then finish the paper with a decorative surface treatment, such as antiquing, shown here.

Computer Lettering Variables

To design text specifically for your project, tailor the look of your lettering by experimenting with the following variables. Most of these variables can be accessed on the tool bar, typically located toward the top of the computer screen.

Font style: There are numerous fonts available on most computer programs. If you're looking for more, several Web sites allow you to download fonts—many at no charge. In addition, most fonts offer further options, such as *italics*, **boldface** and <u>underlining</u>.

Type size: The impact of letters or words can be changed dramatically by adjusting the type size.

Color: Looking for something more exciting than the standard black and white? Change the color of the type, the background or both.

Placement: If you are creating text for a specific area, consider how word placement will affect the design. Typically, text appears flush left, but it can also be centered, justified or placed flush right.

Spacing: If you're working within a limited space, letters and words can often be expanded or condensed to fit. *Kerning*, for example, allows you to place two adjacent letters closer together than usual. By playing with the kerning, you can alter the space between letters to improve the look and legibility of the text.

Using the Computer for Lettering Inspiration

The computer is an amazing tool. With a computer, you can not only print letters, characters and words to incorporate into your projects, you can also search for—and find—an astonishing amount of information. Looking for the perfect quote about food and wine, love and marriage, or children and families? There are hundreds of sites on the World Wide Web where you can find clever sayings. On many sites, these are sorted by theme, so it's easy to find what you're looking for. To explore general listings of quotes and sayings, simply enter the keywords *quotes, quotations* and/or *sayings* into a search engine—then let the Internet do the work for you! If you are looking for a more specific theme—love, for example—use the keywords *quotes + love*. There are also translation sites that can immediately translate words and simple quotes into many different languages.

ONE WORD OF CAUTION: Do not rely on your computer's spell-check program to automatically change your errors. Always proofread your text carefully before printing and run a test print before starting the project...or you could end up with "pottled poetry" instead of "bottled poetry," like I did in this project goof-up!

HAND LETTERING

Hand lettering is one of the most basic ways to add words to a project, but it can also be one of the most intimidating. Don't be nervous if you're not a natural calligrapher—it is easier than you may think to letter by hand. For the best results, start with a lettering guide that includes either an alphabet or the specific saying that you are using. Your guide could be a template from the back of this book, a computer-printed document or a sample from another source. Once you have a lettering guide, you can transfer it, trace over it or use it as a reference. Below are some ideas for easy hand lettering.

| **Transfer lettering onto surface** | Use water-erasable transfer paper to transfer the text onto the surface, then paint in the lettering.

| **Trace over lettering pattern** | If your surface is semitransparent like the fabric square shown above, place a copy of the printed lettering under the surface and secure it with low-tack masking tape. Trace over the lettering with fabric paint, a paint pen or a fine paintbrush.

| **Freehand lettering** | Hand letter your design directly onto the surface, as shown in the image at left. If you are nervous about lettering freehand, sketch the words out first with a chalk pencil before tracing over them with a paint pen or fine paintbrush.

tips

~ When working with dimensional paint or paint pens, always make the first stroke on another surface, such as a scrap piece of paper, before proceeding to your project surface.

~ Some surfaces accept corrections better than others. It is very difficult to remove paint from fabric, so use extra caution when painting on fabric.

BRUSH LETTERING

Brush lettering uses the same basic techniques as lettering with a calligraphic pen but is done instead with a brush. With this kind of lettering, you are forming the letters not with a point, as you would with a pencil tip, but with the line created by the chisel tip of the brush. This results in letters with varying line thicknesses. The brush is held at a 45° angle to the paper to form the thick and thin lines characteristic of basic italic lettering. To keep the strokes sharp and uniform, apply only light pressure to the brush. This will keep the brush hairs from becoming distorted.

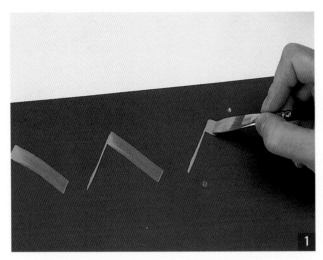 

1 | **Create straight lines** | Holding the chisel point of the brush at a 45° angle to the paper, create a thin line with an upstroke and a broad line with a downstroke. Remember that you are using a line rather than a point to form the thick and thin strokes.

2 | **Create curved lines** | Form a curved stroke in the shape of the letter *C* by starting and ending with a point. Keep the "line," or chisel point of the brush, on the paper at a 45° angle at all times to produce perfect strokes.

3 | **Create reverse-curved lines** | Use the same technique as step 2 to make identical strokes in the reverse direction.

4 | **Practice lettering** | Once you are comfortable handling the brush to make the strokes, practice making letters. Create each letter with a series of simple strokes, pulling every stroke toward you. In many sample chisel-point alphabets, such as the one on page 119, there are arrows and numbers accompanying the letters to indicate the order and direction of the strokes. Use these guidelines to practice lettering until you feel at ease with the process. If possible, practice on paper that is a similar color and texture to your project surface.

Rubber Stamping

Rubber stamps provide another simple and versatile way of lettering your craft projects.

With so many alphabet styles, stamp sizes and ink pad colors, you can customize your lettering to fit any project, from the whimsical to the elegant. Before starting your project, practice on scrap paper to master the skill of stamping.

1 | **Ink stamp** | Ink the stamp by "walking," or tapping, it over the ink pad, moving it up and down lightly across the pad surface several times. Do not press the stamp hard into the pad, as this overinks the stamp and shortens the life of the pad by squeezing out the ink.

2 | **Apply ink to surface** | Determine the placement and spacing of your letters. Whether your surface is flat, like paper, or curved, like the canister shown above, press the stamp with even, downward pressure—not rocking it back and forth—to ensure a clean, crisp image.

tips

~ Lettering stamps do not have to be used just to create words. You can also use text and script stamps as design elements in compositions.

~ Use specialty inks created especially for slick, nonporous surfaces when stamping surfaces such as the stainless steel canister pictured above.

~ It is easier to stamp a curved surface, such as the canister, with smaller stamps.

~ Choose an ink pad that has a raised surface so it can be used with any size of stamp.

~ Store your ink pads upside down to keep the ink fresh on the surface.

3 | **Clean stamp** | When you're finished with the stamp, dab it with stamp cleaner. Be sure to use the proper cleaning fluid recommended for the type of ink you are using. (Do not substitute household cleaners as they can permanently damage the stamp.) Then, gently scrub it clean on a stamp cleaning pad. Press the stamp onto a stack of paper towels to remove the ink and excess cleaner. Make sure the stamp is completely dry before making another image.

STAMPING ON POLYMER CLAY

Stamps can be used for more than applying ink to surfaces. They are also great tools for creating fabulous impressions and textures in polymer clay. Stamped clay is always an exciting medium for lettered ornamentation, whether you're using polymer clay as the primary surface of your project or to make accent pieces for your finished product. For general guidelines and information about working with polymer clay, see page 21.

1 | **Roll out sheet** | With even pressure, roll out conditioned polymer clay on a ceramic tile with an acrylic rod. Roll the clay into an even sheet ⅛" (3mm) thick. You can also use a pasta machine to roll out the clay. (Never use the same pasta machine for both food and polymer clay; if using a machine, designate it for polymer clay use only.)

2 | **Brush clay sheet with powder** | Lightly brush cornstarch powder onto the surface of the polymer clay until the sheet is covered. This will prevent the clay from sticking to the rubber surface of the stamp.

3 | **Create impression** | Press a lettered texture plate facedown onto the powdered surface of the polymer clay sheet. Roll the acrylic rod across the back of the plate to create a deep impression. If you are using a pasta machine, run the plate and clay through the machine together at the thickest setting. The stamped letters can be cut apart into individual pieces using a clay blade or craft knife.

| **An alternate method** | Instead of using texture plates, you can use separate mounted rubber stamps to individually stamp letter motifs into the clay.

STENCILING

Stenciling is a quick and easy method for repeating lettering patterns on a surface. Beautiful ready-made letter stencils can be purchased at craft stores, or homemade stencils can be designed and cut out by hand. Using brushes or sponges, you can stencil most surfaces with paint or ink. Note that the main reason that paint bleeds under the stencil edges is not because the stencil isn't secured properly, but because the brush or the sponge is loaded too heavily with paint. Always make sure that your brush or sponge has the appropriate amount of paint on it before stenciling.

As you are stenciling, keep *interior openings* and *bridges* in mind. Interior openings occur in letters like *A*, *B* and *D*, where there is an enclosed space within the letter. Because most stencils cannot block out the space, you'll have to "create" the interior opening by adding or removing paint after stenciling the letter. Bridges are the blocked-out sections within each letter that reinforce the stencil. When paint or ink is applied over the stencil, the bridge area remains unpainted. To complete the letters, you can close the bridges by hand with paint or ink.

Stenciling with paint and a brush

When stenciling with a brush, the loaded brush is moved up and down on top of the stencil, gradually filling in the stencil design with a stippled effect. For this reason, this technique is sometimes called *stipple stenciling*. Use stencil brushes, which have short, stiff, firmly packed bristles, cut flat at the ends. They are designed to withstand the pouncing motion and to hold a good amount of paint for minimal reloading. Buy the best quality brushes for repeated use and professional-looking results.

1 | **Load brush** | Cut three or four paper towels into quarters, then layer the quarters into a single stack. Load the stencil brush with paint and work the loaded brush in a circular motion onto the paper towel to remove any excess paint.

2 | **Brush paint over stencil** | Place the stencil over the area you wish to paint. Secure it with low-tack masking tape, or hold it firmly in position with your fingers. Mask off the flanking stencil openings with self-adhesive note paper. Apply the paint by pouncing the brush up and down over the stencil openings.

3 | **Touch up** | After the stenciling is complete, touch up the stenciled letters by using a fine paintbrush to connect the unpainted bridges. This gives the letters a less stenciled look.

Stenciling with a sponge

Sponges can also be used to stencil paint onto a surface. Effective and economical, stencil sponges are made of dense foam and are designed to apply a thin, even layer of paint without allowing paint to seep underneath the stencil edges. Just make sure that the sponge is not overloaded before stenciling. You can wash and reuse the sponges or dispose of them after use. Wedge-shaped makeup sponges work equally well.

I **Load sponge and apply paint** I Cut three or four paper towels into quarters, then layer the quarters into a single stack. Load a dense-foam stencil sponge or a wedge-shaped makeup sponge with paint. Pounce the loaded sponge up and down on the paper towel to remove the excess paint and work the paint into the sponge. Place the stencil on the surface and, with an up-and-down dabbing motion, apply the paint through the stencil. When finished, touch up any bridges as necessary with the same paint and a fine paintbrush.

Stenciling with ink and a brush

Using an ink pad and a brush to stencil a design is not unlike using paint and a brush, except instead of pouncing the brush up and down, you scrub the brush with a circular movement called *rouging*. For ink stenciling, I prefer stubby no. 8 and no. 10 fabric brushes with white nylon bristles. It is difficult to overload these brushes, which means less color leakage under the stencil. Use one brush for each color group: for example, one brush for reds and pinks, one for shades of greens, and so on. The ink pad can be dye or pigment ink. One benefit of using ink pads is that you can match the colors exactly if you are using rubber stamps on the project.

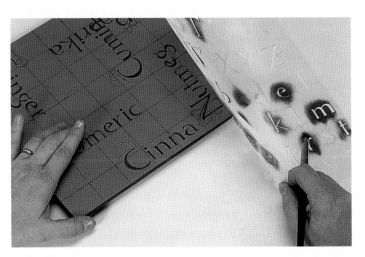

I **Load brush and rouge ink** I Place the stencil over the area you wish to stencil, securing it with low-tack masking tape or holding it firmly in position with your fingers. Load the brush by pouncing it up and down onto the ink pad. Use a circular scrubbing motion to apply the ink through the stencil. When finished, touch up any bridges as necessary with the same ink and a fine, stiff paintbrush. When you use ink, fix the stenciled design with a light coat of sealer spray before varnishing.

Cleaning stencils

To increase the life of your stencils, be sure to clean them soon after using them. Do not wash hand-cut stencils made from freezer paper, like the stencils used in the *Baby Memory Box* project (pages 78–83), as they will disintegrate. The slight buildup of paint over time actually makes hand-cut paper stencils stronger.

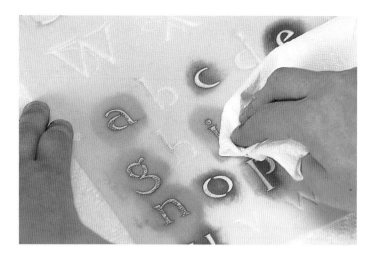

| **Wipe away ink and scrub away paint** | To remove ink from stencils, lay the stencil flat on a dry paper towel and wipe it carefully with another dry paper towel, as shown. To remove acrylic paint from a stencil, lay the stencil flat in a sink, then run warm water over it as you gently scrub away the paint with a surgical scrub brush or a stencil cleaning brush with soft nylon bristles.

Dealing with interior spaces

There are different ways to deal with the interior spaces of letters. Ready-made stencils generally include openings for the interior spaces, placed on the stencil sheet close to the letter to which it belongs. Choose the technique that works best for your specific project.

| **Add paint to create interior space** | If you make your own stencils, keep the leftover "negative" letters that you cut out from the freezer paper. After stenciling, align the paper letter shape directly on top of the stenciled letters, then secure the paper letter to the surface with low-tack masking tape. Load a brush or sponge with the same paint used for the background color, then pounce the loaded brush or sponge up and down onto the surface to fill in the letters' interior openings.

| **Remove paint to create interior space** | On some surfaces, such as the mirror pictured above, you can create the interior space by "erasing" the paint. While the paint is still wet, align the stencil for the interior shape over the letter, then remove the paint through the opening with a cotton swab. If your stencil does not include an opening for the interior space, you can swab off the paint freehand.

EMBOSSING METAL

Embossing words onto metal is a simple technique that yields flashy results. You can cut and emboss metal panels, then add them to your projects as decorative embellishments. I get fantastic results using thin aluminum sheeting for the embossing surface.

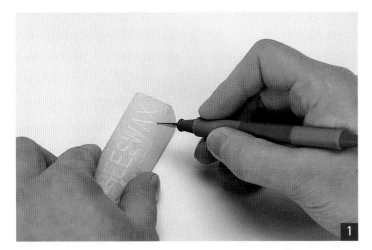

1 | **Lubricate stylus tip** | For embossing metal, the embossing stylus tip should be lubricated so it glides easily. Lubricate the stylus by rubbing the tip along a block of beeswax. If you do not have beeswax, run the stylus tip back and forth along a sheet of waxed paper.

2 | **Emboss metal surface** | Place a smooth metal sheet on a foam pad, such as an embossing pad or a mousepad. With low-tack masking tape, attach a photocopy or a tracing of the pattern to the metal sheet. Lightly trace over the pattern with the stylus tip to emboss the metal sheet beneath.

3 | **Check embossing** | Lift the masking tape on one side and lift the paper to check your embossing on the metal sheet. The lines should be only slightly embossed but easily readable. If you are satisfied with the embossing, reattach the tape and continue tracing with the stylus until the entire pattern is completely embossed.

4 | **Emboss back of sheet** | Remove the pattern paper and turn the metal sheet over. Using the lightly embossed lines as a guide, firmly emboss the reversed word with the stylus.

5 | **Highlight front of sheet** | Flip the metal sheet back over and outline the embossed letters with the stylus. This will give the word a cleaner and deeper embossed appearance.

Basic Crafting Techniques

In the following pages, you'll find descriptions of a few basic crafting techniques used throughout the book. You can use these techniques—basecoating, working with polymer clay, découpaging, antiquing paper and applying a polymer coating—for more than just lettering projects. These techniques can be applied to all sorts of creative craft projects. Familiarize yourself with the techniques, and use this section as a resource when needed.

APPLYING A BASECOAT

A basecoat ensures a smooth finish, ideal for further surface techniques, from transferring patterns to découpaging. For the best results, use a basecoating brush, a ½"–1" (12mm–3cm) brush with flat bristles.

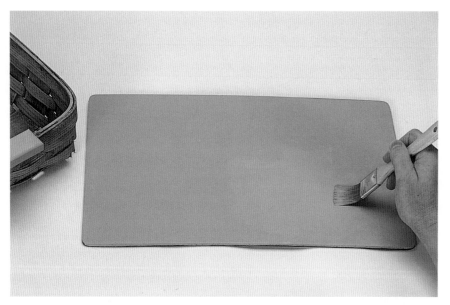

| **Paint, sand, paint** | Seal the wood if desired (see *Tip*, below). Apply the first coat of acrylic paint with a basecoating brush to evenly cover the surface. Allow the paint to dry completely. When dry, sand the painted surface well with 100-grit sandpaper. This results in a very smooth surface, as the moisture in the acrylic paint tends to make the wood fibers come out. Add another coat of paint on top of the sanded, dust-free surface, and, if needed, apply a third coat of paint to cover the surface evenly and reduce the appearance of patches or brush marks.

If your wooden surface has any knots or rough patches, you can seal the dust-free surface of the wood with an acrylic sealer before applying the paint. Let the sealant dry completely before proceeding.

WORKING WITH POLYMER CLAY

Polymer clay can be molded, sculpted and baked to create all kinds of objects. With proper conditioning, baking and finishing, you'll get results that are sure to impress! All you need to mold and sculpt polymer clay are simple household tools and an oven to fire the clay at a low temperature. If you are new to this medium, refer to the tips below for some helpful hints.

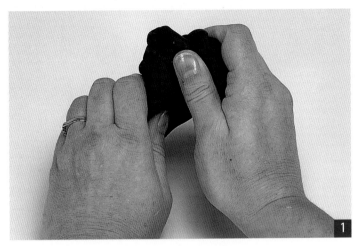 

1 I **Condition polymer clay** I Before starting your polymer clay project, the clay must first be conditioned. Condition a block of clay by working it with your hands until it is soft and pliable.

2 I **Roll out sheet** I With even pressure, roll out the conditioned clay on a ceramic tile with an acrylic rod. Roll the clay into an even sheet approximately ⅛" (3mm) thick. You can also use a pasta machine to roll out the clay, but never use the same pasta machine for both food and polymer clay. If using a machine, designate it for polymer clay use only.

tips

~ Never mix utensils used for food with those used for polymer clay. Clearly mark all your polymer clay tools "for craft use only."

~ Work on a large ceramic tile. It offers a cool, smooth surface and can be placed in the oven to hold the polymer clay while baking.

~ When creating a polymer clay sheet, roll out the clay with an acrylic rod. These rollers can be found anywhere polymer clay is sold. Unlike wooden rolling pins, acrylic rods are designed to prevent the clay from sticking. Wooden rollers will not only cause clay to stick but also will add an unwanted rough texture to the surface. A pasta machine can be used to roll out clay, but these machines are better for conditioning and producing very thin sheets of clay.

~ Follow the manufacturer's directions carefully for baking the polymer clay. Generally, polymer clays are baked in a low 275° F (135°C) oven for 30 minutes. To avoid burning the clay, a separate oven thermometer is recommended to make sure the oven is at the right temperature. It is generally okay to bake the clay a little longer, but never in a hotter oven.

~ You can bake your projects in your home oven, but a small toaster oven dedicated to polymer clay baking works best. For larger items, such as the *Caffeine Canister* described on pages 88–91, a toaster oven is too small. Bake these larger items in your home oven.

DÉCOUPAGING

Découpage—from the French word *découper*, meaning *to cut out*—is the technique of decorating a surface with paper cutouts. For découpage images, you can use specialty découpage paper, decorative scrapbooking paper, self-adhesive stickers, images from magazines, wrapping paper, color photocopies and specially made paper kits that include coordinating papers and images.

1 | **Select elements and cut out** | After selecting your découpage components, cut out each one, leaving space around the perimeter. Then, cut precisely along the perimeter of the image or text, moving the paper, not the scissors. As you cut, hold the scissors at a 45° angle to the paper. This creates a tiny beveled edge, which will help the paper stay glued snugly against the surface. Use a craft knife to cut out any interior forms.

2 | **Arrange pieces** | Collect all your paper components. Play with the pieces, placing them as desired on the surface. Do not be afraid to overlap pieces, leave blank spaces and run pieces off the edge of the surface. Place all text components parallel to each other for easy reading. Continue arranging the components until you have a composition that you like.

3 | **Glue pieces down** | Using a sponge brush, apply a thin coat of découpage medium to the back of each piece, covering it completely. Glue down the larger pieces first, then add the smaller ones, lifting and tucking pieces as necessary to overlap. Images that go right to the edges can be wrapped around the surface, as shown, and glued to the back.

4 | **Seal with découpage medium** | Once everything has been glued down, make sure all the pieces are flat. Brush découpage medium over the surface with a sponge brush. Use your fingers to smooth out any bubbles. Again, make sure everything is flat, pressing down any pieces as necessary. Once the first coat of medium has dried, add a second coat.

ANTIQUING PAPER

This is a fabulous technique for giving paper surfaces an aged appearance. I prefer a solution of ¼ cup (60ml) instant coffee granules and 2 cups (474ml) hot water, which results in hues from cream to dark walnut. Other solutions will create different effects. Strong brewed tea, for example, can be used for ecru to sepia tones. I have even mixed instant fruit drink powders (the type with no sugar added) with water and a splash of vinegar for a wide range of interesting colors. To antique the paper, simply brush or sponge the solution directly onto the surface and let it dry. The antiquing solution tends to dry dark, so make sure that deep puddles don't cover any important words or images.

Look closely at the two sides of a sea sponge. Before the sponge was harvested, one side was attached to the rock, while the other side faced out toward the water. After working with sponges, you'll notice that each side creates a different look. You can achieve a finely detailed effect from the sea side and a larger, rougher texture from the rock side.

| Brush on solution |

Place the paper to be antiqued on top of a sheet of waxed paper. Using a large brush, apply the solution to the paper, over the text and images. Allow puddles to form on the paper. This will create depth and enhance the look of the project. Allow the solution to dry.

| Sponge on solution |

Place the paper to be antiqued on top of a sheet of waxed paper. Use a fine sea sponge to apply the solution over the words and images (see *Tip*, at right). You can leave some of the paper untouched or dab off excess solution as desired. Allow the solution to dry.

Crafting with Paper

Découpaging and antiquing techniques involve the use of paper and paper craft supplies. When it comes to crafting with paper, you have many exciting options, including scrapbooking supplies and ephemera.

For découpage, scrapbooking supplies are a great find. The growing popularity of scrapbooking has given rise to the availability of beautiful decorative paper as well as different lettering and alphabet embellishments. Paper craft supplies include dimensional stickers, metal letter studs, typewriter keys, resin letters, precut paper letters, laser-cut metal letters and more. These can be found at your local craft stores.

If the look of aged paper appeals to you, you can simulate that look using the **Antiquing Paper** technique, described above. Also consider incorporating **ephemera** into your projects. Ephemera, which is printed material of passing interest, includes handwritten love letters, pages from books, and old documents. If you can't find any heirloom pieces in your attic, search secondhand or antique stores for old letters, postcards and family records. Always make and use color photocopies of valuable pieces rather than including the originals in your projects.

APPLYING A POLYMER COATING

Polymer coating is a liquid plastic coating that can be poured onto a variety of surfaces. Once it cures, the coating provides a thick, permanent, waterproof, high-gloss surface. I use Envirotex Lite, a high-quality, user-friendly brand of polymer coating that has a low odor. The coating comes in two parts, a resin and a hardener. When equal parts of resin and hardener are mixed together, they react chemically to form the plastic coating. Approximately 4 ounces (118ml) of Envirotex Lite polymer coating will cover 1 square foot (.9 square meter) of your project.

The process of coating an object requires a few supplies. In addition to the coating itself, you'll need paper or plastic disposable cups (for supporting objects above the work surface), disposable latex gloves, waxed paper, a plastic disposable measuring cup (for measuring and mixing), wooden stir sticks and disposable glue brushes. Before beginning, raise your project above the work surface by resting it on inverted disposable cups; this will allow the coating to drip freely off the sides for an even application.

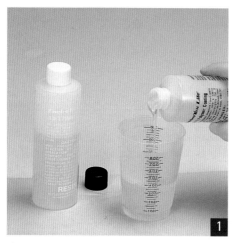 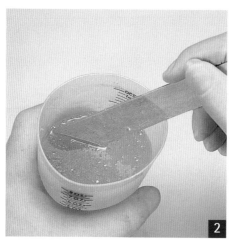 

1 | **Measure resin and hardener** | Lay several sheets of waxed paper over your work surface. Elevate your project about 2" (5cm) over the waxed paper on paper or plastic cups. Wearing disposable gloves, measure the resin and hardener in a single disposable plastic measuring cup. Measure exact amounts by volume; do not try to guess, or your coating will be soft and sticky. Measure out only the amount you need for the item to be coated.

2 | **Stir mixture** | Use a wooden stir stick to vigorously stir the resin-hardener mixture for two minutes until thoroughly blended. Continually scrape the sides and bottom while mixing to avoid soft or tacky spots on your finished piece. Do not worry about bubbles; they are a sign that you are mixing well.

3 | **Pour mixture** | Immediately after mixing the resin coating, pour it over the surface of the elevated project in a circular pattern. Start close to the edge and work toward the center. This will allow the coating to level out.

4 | Spread coating | Help spread the polymer coating where necessary with a disposable glue brush. Be careful not to spread the coating too thin, or the surface will be wavy. You have approximately 25 minutes of working time before the coating starts to set up. About 30 minutes after pouring, wipe away any drips along the bottom edge of your project with a glue brush. Repeat after another 30 minutes to minimize drips.

5 | Eliminate air bubbles | Within 10 minutes of pouring, the air bubbles created while mixing will rise to the surface. Gently exhale (do not blow) across the surface to get rid of them. The carbon dioxide in your breath will break the bubbles. On large surfaces, use a heat gun or small propane torch to remove the air bubbles. Do not hold the heating tool closer than 3"–4" (8cm–10cm) to the surface, since it's carbon dioxide, not the heat, that creates results.

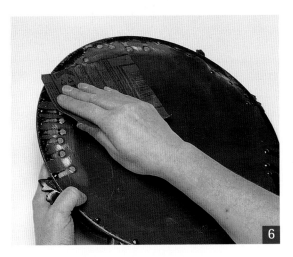

6 | Cure and clean surface | Allow the coated item to cure overnight in a warm, dust-free room. The polymer coating cures to the touch in about 12 hours and cures fully in 72 hours. After the item has cured fully, remove the drips from the underside of the surface by sanding. A circular sanding attachment on a hand drill works well, but you can also sand by hand using 100-grit sandpaper.

Note: You don't necessarily have to sand off the drips. If you pour the coating evenly, your drips will be even and level. This will provide a nice rest for some objects, such as coasters and trivets.

tips

~ Polymer coating is chemically inert once it has cured. It becomes completely machineable at that point, making it easy to drill or sand.

~ You can allow the natural high-gloss shine of the polymer coating to remain on the surface, or you can create a matte finish by polishing it with fine steel wool or by spraying on a coat of exterior clear matte varnish.

~ Protect the cured coating from scratches and marks by rubbing the surface with carnauba car wax.

~ If you plan to finish a découpaged piece with a polymer coating, first seal the surface with two thin coats of white glue. The glue seal must be completely dry before applying the polymer coating. If paper is not sealed properly, the resin from the coating will seep underneath and create a dark spot.

~ When I give handmade gifts that have been coated, I send along a care card. Here is a sample of a care card included with a set of coasters:

~ COASTER CARE CARD ~

THESE COASTERS ARE HEAT-RESISTANT, WATERPROOF AND ALCOHOL-PROOF • CLEAN WITH A SOFT, DAMP CLOTH. CARNAUBA CAR WAX WILL PROLONG THE LIFE OF THE SURFACE AND CLEAN SMUDGES AND FINGERPRINTS • OBJECTS, WHEN LEFT ON THE SURFACE FOR A PERIOD OF TIME, MAY LEAVE IMPRESSIONS. THEY WILL DISAPPEAR IN A FEW HOURS AT NORMAL ROOM TEMPERATURES.

The Lettering Projects

Whether you use letters as a design element or to form words and sayings, the addition of lettering can set your crafted projects apart from all others. In the following pages, you'll find a wide selection of home décor projects that illustrate the different effects you can achieve with lettering. Some projects are casual, fun and playful; others are sophisticated, romantic and refined. In all of the projects, it is the lettering style that gives each its distinctive look. The perfect lettering style for your craft project is always within your reach, and this book aims to inspire you with many possibilities!

A materials list is provided at the beginning of each project in this section, including a reference to the relevant patterns, templates and guides in the back of the book. Because the projects call for an array of techniques, the materials that you'll need will vary from project to project. Lettering tools range from paint and paintbrush to computer printer, with everything from stencils to rubber stamps in between. The techniques used are also listed at the beginning of each project. These techniques are explained in detail in the introductory section, pages 8–25. Before starting a project, you can review the technique explanation on the pages indicated. For some of the projects, you'll also find a section called *In Other Words*, a list of suggested words and sayings to use. Feel free to look for your own favorite sayings to fit the project theme.

> The perfect lettering style for your craft project is always within your reach, and this book aims to inspire you with many possibilities!

Above all, these projects are designed to be enjoyable for both novice and veteran crafters. You don't have to be an artist with perfect penmanship to master the art of lettering. With these projects, you'll learn tricks for lettering that will give you the confidence of an expert artisan. So, relax, have fun and express your creativity with letters while creating beautiful objects for your home.

Nothing complements a photograph of a smiling face better than this cheerful frame.

Smile! silver frame

Decorated with embossed tags and metal scrapbook words, this frame features fun and quirky lettering—perfect for a theme of smiles and laughter. To accentuate the whimsical feeling, the embossed letters bounce to form each word. The eye-catching effect of embossed metal is easy to create and sure to draw rave reviews. Once you know how to do it, you can use the embossing technique to make all kinds of lettering embellishments.

MATERIALS AND TOOLS

7" x 9" (18cm x 23cm) wooden frame, with 3½" x 5½" (9cm x 14cm) opening

photocopy of *Smile! Word Templates*, page 118

Delta Ceramcoat acrylic paint
　Metallic Silver

basecoating brush

laser-cut metal words, available at scrapbooking and craft stores

100-grit sandpaper

thin metal (aluminum) sheeting

metal burnisher

embossing stylus with fine embossing tip

beeswax (or sheet of waxed paper)

embossing pad (or foam pad or mousepad)

plastic shape templates, square and rectangle

decorative-edged scissors, such as miniscallop, scallop, minipinking and pinking

multipack of miniature square accent mirrors

liquid permanent adhesive

armature wire

wire cutters

flat pliers

OPTIONAL: vise

TECHNIQUES USED IN THIS PROJECT

Applying a Basecoat (page 20)
Embossing Metal (page 19)

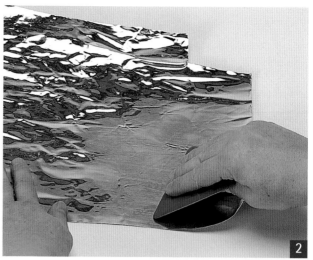

1 | **Basecoat frame** | Basecoat the wooden frame with silver metallic acrylic paint, sanding between each application of paint, as directed in the *Applying a Basecoat* instructions on page 20.

2 | **Burnish metal sheet** | Place the thin metal sheet on a flat surface. Using a metal burnisher, smooth out the sheet to eliminate all wrinkles and creases.

3 | **Use pattern to emboss metal sheet** | Photocopy the word templates in the back of the book (page 118), then cut out each individual photocopied template. Use the templates to emboss words on the metal sheet, following the *Embossing Metal* instructions on page 19.

4 | **Finish embossing words** | Continue embossing all the words until you have enough tags to embellish the surface of the frame: about five or six for this 7" x 9" (18cm x 23cm) frame.

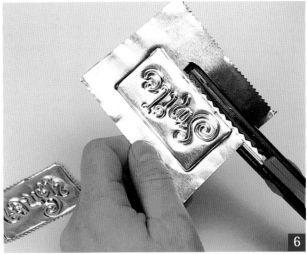

5 | **Emboss border** | Using square and rectangular templates, trace a border around each word with the embossing stylus. If you don't have a template, emboss the border lines by running the stylus tip along a metal ruler.

6 | **Cut out embossed tags** | Cut out each embossed word tag with a pair of decorative-edged scissors. Use a different edge for each tag, if desired. Cut just outside, not over, the border lines.

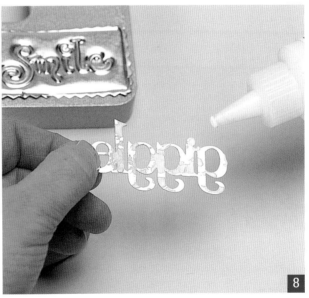

7 | **Plan design** | Plan your design by laying out all the design elements—the embossed tags, the laser-cut metal words and the miniature square accent mirrors—as desired on the frame face. When arranging the elements, it is a good idea to lay out the larger objects first, as shown, followed by the smaller objects.

8 | **Glue on tags and words** | Use permanent adhesive to glue the embossed metal tags on the frame as you placed them in step 7. Carefully dab the permanent adhesive onto the back of the laser-cut words, then press each onto the frame in the desired position.

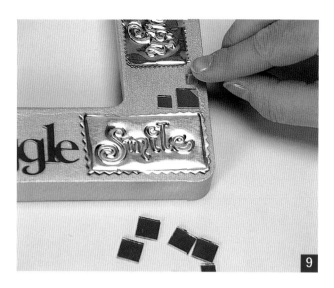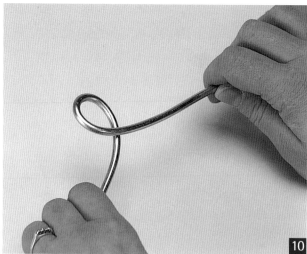

9 | **Glue on mirror accents** | Finish the frame by gluing the miniature accent mirrors in place. Again, carefully dab the permanent adhesive onto the back of the mirrors, then press onto the frame as desired.

10 | **Cut and bend armature wire** | Using wire cutters, cut a piece of armature wire 36" (91cm) long. Bend the wire in half, making a loop at the center.

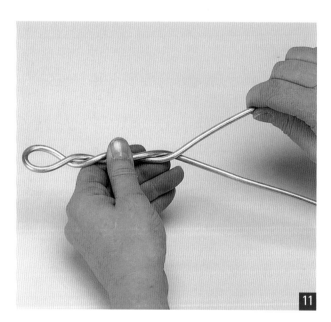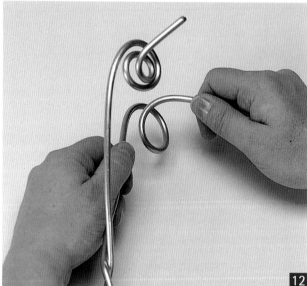

11 | **Twist wire** | Starting at the base of the loop, twist the two sides of the wire together until you have about 3"–4" (8cm–10cm) of twisted wire.

12 | **Spiral ends into curlicues** | Spiral each end of the wire several times to form a curlicue. This takes muscle; it may be easier to secure the wire in a vise or have somebody hold the wire while you twist it.

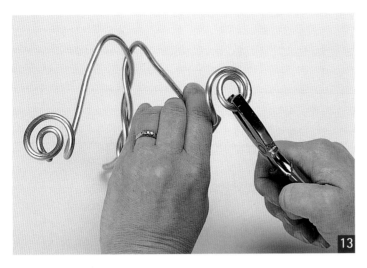

13 | Finish easel | Use flat pliers to manipulate the wire, twisting and bending it until you have a self-standing easel that will accommodate your frame.

IN OTHER WORDS

Use your choice of words, phrases and sayings to embellish the *Smile! Silver Frame*. Looking for a little inspiration? Here are some ideas you may find helpful:

- Laugh
- Smile
- Grin
- Chuckle
- Giggle
- Beam
- Chortle

The Finished Look

Trim a favorite photograph to fit inside the frame opening. For a frame backing, cut a piece of cardboard to the size of the opening. Use small nails or framer's points to secure the photo and the cardboard in the frame.

Variation: metal tags

These metal tags, decorated with wire and beads, make fantastic gift tags, scrapbook embellishments or card ornaments.

Bring a simple terra cotta flowerpot to life by decorating it with your favorite garden-inspired expression.

Celtic lettered flowerpot

Equipped with a series of flat paintbrushes and the alphabet guide in the back of this book, you can create beautiful chisel-point lettering in a variety of sizes. The Celtic-style alphabet used in this project is a form of *uncial majuscule* lettering. *Uncial*, meaning *inch* in Latin, was the term appointed to this style in the sixth century. Found in illuminated manuscripts of the Middle Ages, the uncial style is still associated with the magic of the ancient Celtic world. This style is perfect for beginners who are just trying their hand at chisel-point lettering, as it offers simple letter structure.

MATERIALS AND TOOLS

terra cotta flowerpot

Celtic Alphabet Guide, page 119

Delta Ceramcoat acrylic paint
- Eucalyptus
- Metallic Gold
- Red Iron Oxide
- Seminole Green

acrylic brush-on sealer

acrylic thinner

acrylic spray sealer

satin acrylic varnish

brushes
- wide brushes for basecoating and varnishing
- small flat, chisel-tip brushes for lettering
- small round paintbrush

Brush-Up paper (see *Tip*, page 36)

terra cotta-colored card-weight paper

rubber bands

metallic gold paint pens or markers
- chisel-tip (calligraphy)
- round-tip

paper towels

TECHNIQUES USED IN THIS PROJECT

Brush Lettering (page 13)

1 | **Practice lettering on paper** | Use a paintbrush and clean water to practice lettering strokes on Brush-Up paper, following the *Brush Lettering* instructions on page 13 and the *Celtic Alphabet Guide* on page 119. The lettering will disappear after a few minutes, leaving a blank surface for more practice (see *Tip*, below).

2 | **Practice strokes on terra cotta-colored paper** | Using a flat brush and Eucalyptus acrylic paint, practice making strokes on paper that has the same terra cotta color and slick surface as the flowerpot. Continue to refer to the *Brush Lettering* guidelines on page 13 as necessary.

BRUSH-UP PAPER: Sometimes called "Zen paper," Brush-Up paper features a special coated surface that allows you to practice lettering techniques with water instead of paint. Simply wet your brush and begin lettering. Don't worry if you make a mistake; the paper dries without any trace of water spots, so it can be reused over and over.

3 | **Practice lettering on terra cotta-colored paper** | On the same kind of paper used in step 2, practice brush lettering in the Celtic style, continuing to refer to the alphabet guide on page 119 as necessary. Practice until you feel at ease with the lettering process.

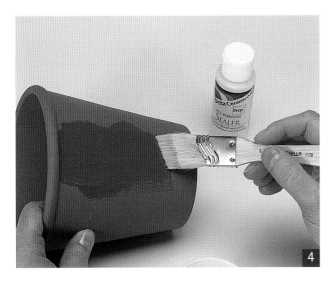 

4 | **Apply layer of sealer** | Brush one coat of acrylic sealer onto the exterior surface of the flowerpot. This gives the pot a slicker surface so that your brush glides over it, making smooth strokes. Once the surface is coated with sealer, you can use a paper towel to wipe away any mistakes that you may make when lettering the pot.

5 | **Paint pot interior** | Coat the interior and the rim of the pot with Metallic Gold acrylic paint. For an even finish, apply at least two coats of paint.

6 | **Lay out lettering** | Wrap a rubber band around the pot to provide a straight line for lettering. Mix a very light wash, consisting of Eucalyptus acrylic paint and acrylic thinner. With a small flat paintbrush, use this wash to lightly map out your lettering on the pot, adding another rubber band for each line. If you make a mistake, wipe off the paint with a slightly damp paper towel; allow the surface to dry, then repaint the lettering.

7 | **Paint lettering** | When you are satisfied with the lettering, go over the wash with undiluted Eucalyptus acrylic paint. If paint straight from the bottle seems too thick, dilute it with a drop of acrylic thinner. If you add acrylic thinner to the paint, you may need to solidify the strokes by adding one or two more layers.

8 | **Touch up lettering** | Sharpen all the corners of the lettering with a small round paintbrush. Allow the paint to dry.

9 | **Shadow lettering** | Use a flat paintbrush to shadow the letters with Red Iron Oxide acrylic paint. By adding a subtle shadow to the lettering strokes, you give the letters a polished look and conceal any residual wash from step 6. Allow the paint to dry.

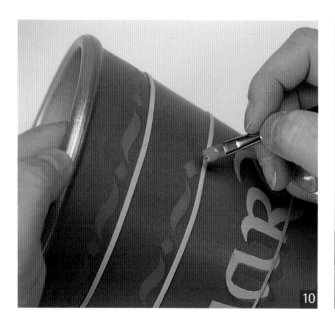

10 | **Apply decorative accents** | Wrap two rubber bands around the top half of the pot, spacing them about 1" (3cm) apart, for two lines of decorative embellishments. Using a flat paintbrush, apply a dot-and-dash motif around the pot with Seminole Green acrylic paint. Apply simple strokes as you did with the lettering, holding the brush at a 45° angle to the surface of the pot. Allow the paint to dry.

11 | **Add diamonds and dots** | Wrap four more rubber bands around the pot to make a series of straight lines for additional embellishments. Use a metallic gold chisel-tip paint pen to add a decorative motif of diamonds and a metallic gold round-tip paint pen to add dots. Complete four rows of these decorative accents. As you are adding decorative accents to the surface, always keep in mind the space that remains. Look ahead frequently to anticipate how much space you have left, then space the embellishments appropriately. Allow the pen paint to dry.

12 | Spray and varnish pot | Apply a very light misting of spray sealer over the pot. (This will prevent the paint from running when you apply varnish.) Allow the sealer to dry. With a wide paintbrush, apply satin varnish to the exterior surface of the pot.

Note: The paint tends to darken a shade after you apply the varnish.

IN OTHER WORDS

Use your choice of words, phrases and sayings to embellish the *Celtic Lettered Flowerpot*. Looking for a little inspiration? Here are some ideas you may find helpful:

- Time began in a garden.
- Love makes a garden grow.
- May all your weeds be wildflowers.
- Nurture nature.
- Earth laughs in flowers.
- Walk on the rainbow trail.
- May your days be filled with rainbows.

The Finished Look

Use the finished flowerpot as a beautiful garden accent, or add a plant and present it to a friend. To turn the painted pot into a fancy waterproof vase, coat the inside with a polymer coating as described on pages 24–25.

Variation: painted tray

Using the same acrylic colors and lettering style, create this matching wooden tray to complement the flowerpot.

When you choose a lettering style for your project, consider how it fits with the overall theme.

Découpaged wine tray

For this tray, I used the computer font called *Papyrus*. Its casual but sophisticated look is perfect for the wine-and-grapes motif. With so many fonts available on today's computer software programs, all kinds of fabulous lettering styles are possible. You have many design options for this project, so feel free to choose any font and decorative paper that strikes your fancy. I selected a paper with a cursive script design, which provides a nice background for the printed text.

MATERIALS AND TOOLS

round pressed-wood tray, 13½" (34cm) diameter

two handles for tray (cabinet handles will work)

computer (with Papyrus or other desired font) and printer

Delta Ceramcoat acrylic paint
- Chocolate Cherry
- Metallic Copper

gel stain medium

satin découpage medium

satin or matte acrylic varnish

brushes
- brushes for basecoating and varnishing
- no. 6 flat paintbrush
- sponge brush

sea sponge

découpage paper with grapes and vine leaves
{GORGEOUS GRAPES BY PLAID ENTERPRISES, INC.}

decorative or scrapbook paper with cursive text motif
{GORGEOUS GRAPES BY PLAID ENTERPRISES, INC.}

wine labels or wine-label clip art

100-grit sandpaper

craft knife

scissors

thin white glue

waxed paper

Envirotex Lite polymer coating

polymer coating supplies
- disposable plastic measuring cup
- small disposable plastic cups
- wooden stir sticks
- disposable glue brushes
- disposable latex gloves
- heat gun

OPTIONAL: palm or contour sander

TECHNIQUES USED IN THIS PROJECT

Applying a Basecoat (page 20)
Using a Computer to Generate Lettering (pages 10–11)
Découpaging (page 22)
Applying a Polymer Coating (pages 24–25)

1 I **Basecoat tray** I Basecoat the wooden tray with Chocolate Cherry acrylic paint, sanding between each application of paint, as directed in the *Applying a Basecoat* instructions on page 20.

2 I **Begin trimming images** I Select images from the découpage paper to include in your design. Using a craft knife, remove any interior openings such as the gaps between the leaves and stems, as shown.

3 I **Cut out images** I Use a sharp pair of scissors to first cut around the image, leaving a ¼" (6mm) border around the perimeter. Then, holding the scissors at a 45° angle to the paper, move the paper—not the scissors—to cut precisely along the perimeter of the image.

4 I **Create text components** I Use a computer to design and print the wine-related sayings of your choice, referring to the *Using a Computer to Generate Lettering* instructions on pages 10–11 as needed. I used the Papyrus font in a variety of sizes, then printed the text in purple ink on green decorative paper; you can alter the font, size and color as desired. Crop each saying by ripping the paper around the text. Tear the paper toward you rather than away from you to give the paper a nice white deckled edge. When you are finished, tear out irregularly shaped pieces and strips from the remaining scraps of paper.

5 | **Paint deckled edges** | Use a no. 6 flat paintbrush to coat the deckled edges of the paper with Metallic Copper acrylic paint, covering all the white parts of the torn areas.

6 | **Cut out wine labels** | Cut out the wine labels of your choice. If the colors of your wine labels do not coordinate with the rest of your text and images, cover them with a glaze made from the basecoat color. To do this, mix equal amounts of gel stain medium and Chocolate Cherry acrylic paint in a small plastic cup. Brush the glaze over the labels, then cut out the labels once the glaze is dry.

7 | **Sponge paint onto tray rim** | Load a natural sea sponge with Metallic Copper acrylic paint, then press the sponge several times onto a piece of waxed paper to work the paint into the sponge. Dab the paint around the rim of the tray for an even, textured application.

8 | **Découpage tray** | Follow the *Découpaging* instructions on page 22 to découpage the tray surface with your images, labels and text components, finishing with two layers of découpage medium. In your composition, keep all the text components parallel but don't be afraid to overlap pieces and run pieces off the edge of the tray.

9 | **Cover with glue** | When the top layer of découpage medium is dry, use a wide paintbrush to apply a coat of thin white glue over the top surface of the tray. Do not be alarmed if the glue appears white when you brush it on; it will dry clear. Allow the glue to dry, then add a second layer of glue. Allow the second layer of glue to dry completely.

10 | **Coat tray with polymer** | When the glue has dried completely, follow the *Applying a Polymer Coating* instructions on pages 24–25 to coat the tray with a thick, waterproof coating. Use a heat gun to eliminate the air bubbles before moving on to the next step.

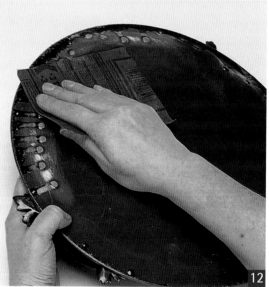

11 | **Add handles** | Immediately after applying and heating the polymer finish, set the two handles directly into the coating. Place one handle on each side of the tray, first resting them on the rim, then pressing them gently into the polymer finish. Periodically check the handles for a few hours to make sure they don't start sliding off the rim. Once the polymer coating begins to cure, the handles will become more secure.

12 | **Cure and sand surface** | Let the tray cure overnight. Once the polymer coating has cured, remove any drips from the bottom of the tray by sanding the surface with a piece of 100-grit sandpaper. You can use a palm sander or a contour sander for speedier sanding.

13 | Repaint and varnish bottom | The sanding process may remove some of the basecoat, so repaint the bottom of the tray with a layer of Chocolate Cherry acrylic paint. Finish by brushing a coat of satin or matte acrylic varnish onto the bottom of the tray. Your drip marks may still be visible, but the paint and varnish will conceal most of them. Allow the varnish to dry completely before using the tray.

IN OTHER WORDS

Use your choice of words, phrases and sayings to embellish the *Découpaged Wine Tray*. Looking for a little inspiration? Here are some ideas you may find helpful:

- Friendship is the wine of life.
- *Bonum vinum laetifical cor hominis.* (Good wine gladdens a person's heart.)
- "Wine is sunlight held together by water." — Galileo
- *In vino veritas.* (In wine there is truth.)
- The noblest of fruits is the grape for in its death comes the wine.
- *Carpe vino.* (Seize the wine.)
- Life is too short to drink cheap wine.

The Finished Look

The polymer coating on this tray makes it a practical, usable surface for serving wine or other refreshments to guests. By using other découpage papers and lettered sayings, you can create your own custom-themed trays for exquisite gifts.

Variation: trivet and coasters

Using the same materials and techniques, découpage several round wooden plaques to make coasters and a matching trivet. Stick cork buttons on the bottom surface of each for added stability.

Covered with an array of decorative letters, this desk set will add flair to any office.

Gilded letter desk set

Lettering doesn't always have to spell out a word or a phrase to have an impact. In this project, letters are fashioned from polymer clay, gilded with metallic powdered pigment, then used as design elements to embellish a pen, a pen holder and other office supplies. Since the design does not call for a sequence of words, you are not limited to one or two particular lettering styles. So, feel free to choose stamps or lettering plates that feature a fun mix of styles and sizes.

MATERIALS AND TOOLS

short glass cylinder jar or vase, 4" (10cm) diameter x 4" (10cm) deep

Bic pen (NOTE: Use a Bic pen with a white barrel, as other pens may melt during baking)

black polymer clay, conditioned

polymer clay tools
  · ceramic tile
  · acrylic rod
  · clay blade or craft knife
  · oven

brushes
  · disposable glue brush
  · soft paintbrush (any size)

alphabet rubber stamps
{VINTAGE ALPHABET BY HERO ARTS}

rubber lettering plate
{CALLIGRAPHIC BACKGROUND PRINTS BY USARTQUEST}

thin white glue

metal ruler

cornstarch powder

gold powdered pigment

waxed paper

OPTIONAL: metal letter opener and metal thumbtacks

TECHNIQUES USED IN THIS PROJECT

Working With Polymer Clay (page 21)
Stamping on Polymer Clay (page 15)

1 | **Prepare jar with glue** | Using a glue brush, apply thin white glue to the exterior surface of the glass jar. This process will help the clay adhere to the slick glass surface. Don't worry if the glue dries as you proceed through the next few steps; the clay will bond to the glue even if it is dry.

2 | **Roll out polymer clay sheet** | Using an acrylic rod, roll out a sheet of conditioned polymer clay on a ceramic tile. Roll the clay into an even sheet approximately 1/8" (3mm) thick.

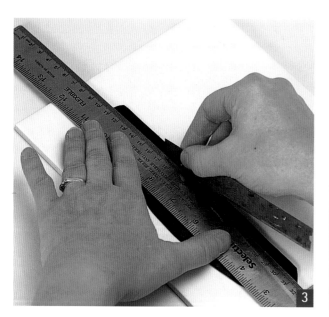

3 | **Cut clay strips** | Position a metal ruler on top of the polymer clay sheet, then use a clay blade to cut four strips of clay, each 3/4" (19mm) wide.

4 | **Apply clay strip to jar** | Apply one of the clay strips to the exterior of the jar along the bottom edge, pressing the clay to the surface as you go. If necessary, apply another strip to complete the bottom trim. Smooth the seam where the ends meet. Reserve the remaining clay strips for steps 10 and 13.

5 | **Create lettered polymer clay sheet** | Using the acrylic rod, roll out another sheet of polymer clay to an even ⅛" (3mm) thickness. Use a rubber lettering plate to impress a lettering design in the clay sheet, following the *Stamping on Polymer Clay* instructions on page 15.

6 | **Trim edges** | Use a clay blade to trim off the uneven edges of the lettered polymer clay sheet. Take the prepared jar and measure from ¼" (6mm) below the rim to the top of the clay strip trim. Use a clay blade to cut the lettered polymer clay sheet to this width.

7 | **Gild lettered sheet** | Gild the clay impression with gold powdered pigment, using your finger to work the powder onto the surface. Lightly brush the surface with a soft paintbrush to remove any excess powder.

8 | **Cover jar with sheet** | Place the gilded sheet around the jar, positioning it flush with the clay strip around the bottom. You may need to create and add another gilded clay sheet if one doesn't fit around the whole jar.

9 | **Join edges** | Join the edges of the sheet(s) to form a seam. Blend the seam, then rub more of the powdered pigment along the joint to unite the edges.

10 | **Add clay strip to rim** | Place the reserved clay strip(s) from step 4 along the top rim of the jar. Press the strip against the glass, up to and slightly over the rim.

11 | **Stamp rim and bake** | Pour out a bit of the powdered pigment onto a sheet of waxed paper. Select your choice of individual letter stamps to create a monogram along the bottom trim. Press each stamp into the clay to make an impression. If desired, first press the stamp into the powder to make a gilded impression. When the jar is finished, bake it in a 275°F (135°C) oven for 30 minutes. (See page 21 for additional baking hints.)

12 | **Cover pen with clay** | Create another sheet of clay, impressed with the lettering plate and gilded with the powdered pigment. Lightly brush the surface with a soft paintbrush to remove any excess powder. With a clay blade, cut the sheet to a piece that will cover the white barrel of a Bic pen, approximately 1" x 4¼" (3cm x 11cm), leaving ¾" (19mm) at the end of the barrel.

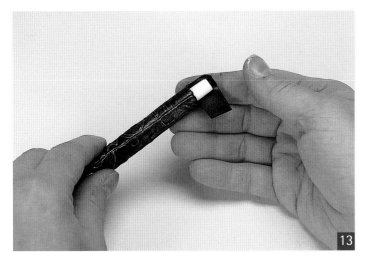

13 | **Bake pen** | Use a clay blade to cut a strip of black polymer clay approximately 1" x ¾" (3cm x 19mm). Apply the strip around the exposed end of the pen barrel and smooth out the seams. Remove the nib and ink cartridge from the pen; set these components aside. Bake the pen, then let it cool completely before replacing the nib and ink cartridge.

The Finished Look

This coordinated, personalized desk set is a great addition to anyone's office décor. For additional accessories, I covered the handle of a metal letter opener and the tops of several thumbtacks with the gilded clay.

Variation: picture frame

Add one more matching piece to the desk set with this lettered picture frame. Simply paint a wooden frame black, cover it with stamped and gilded clay tiles, then bake.

KATELYN

JONATHAN

BROWNING

SCOTT

EST.

LENA

1989

MARIE

A combination of photographs and lettering, these family wall tiles are a unique twist on scrapbooking.

Family wall tiles

A torn photograph and layers of stenciled lettering are incorporated into the design of these faux wall tiles, giving them a collaged look. In this particular project, I've used the tiles to compose a record of my family, documenting our life with a favorite photo, family members' names and the year our home was established. You can adapt the project to make a series of tiles recording your own significant friendships or memorable events. The ochre-colored tiles look so real, nobody will ever guess they are actually made from sheets of foam!

MATERIALS AND TOOLS

1" (3cm) thick Styrofoam sheet(s), enough for two 6" x 6" (15cm x 15cm) pieces, one 7" x 7" (18cm x 18cm) piece and one 6" x 8" (15cm x 20cm) piece

stencils
    script and block monogram letters, with 1" (3cm) large letters and ½" (13mm) small letters
    vine border

Delta Ceramcoat acrylic paint
    Black
    Light Timberline Green
    Pine Green

Delta Texture Magic acrylic paint
    Cashmere
    Metallic Gold
    Sienna
    Vintage Leather

Delta Texture Magic antiquing gel

satin découpage medium

brushes
    stenciling brushes
    stencil cleaning brush
    wide flat brushes
    fine paintbrush

metal ruler

utility knife

palette knife

waxed paper or palette paper

paper towels

low-tack masking tape

self-adhesive note paper

family photograph, preferably black and white

color photocopier

OPTIONAL: Lazertran transfer decal paper

TECHNIQUES USED IN THIS PROJECT
Stenciling (pages 16–18)
Découpaging (page 22)

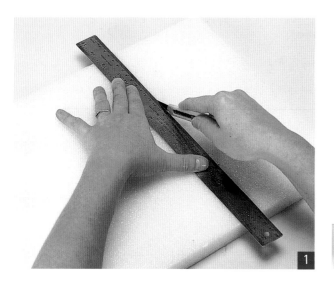

1 | **Cut foam sheet** | Using a metal ruler as a guide, cut the Styrofoam sheet with a utility knife into two 6" x 6" (15cm x 15cm) squares, one 7" x 7" (18cm x 18cm) square and one 6" x 8" (15cm x 20cm) rectangle. The blade will cut but not penetrate all the way through the foam sheet.

2 | **Separate foam pieces** | Separate the foam pieces by snapping the sheet in two along the score line with a downward motion.

3 | **Round corners** | Rock each corner of the foam pieces along a hard surface until all the corners are rounded.

4 | **Apply texture paint** | Squeeze approximately ½ cup (118ml) each of Sienna and Vintage Leather texture paint onto a sheet of waxed paper or palette paper. Use a palette knife to spread the paint across one side of a foam sheet and onto the edges, alternating the two colors. Allow the colors to blend roughly on the surface. Paint the remaining three tiles in the same manner and allow the paint to dry.

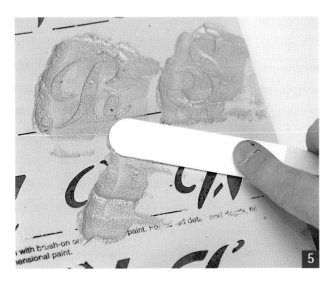

5 | Stencil first layer of words | Place a script stencil over one painted Styrofoam tile, then use a palette knife to spread Metallic Gold texture paint over the stencil openings. Stencil at least three rows of lettering across the tile. Don't be overly cautious with the application; it doesn't matter if some of the paint bleeds under the stencil because the lettering will be covered with the next layer of paint in step 7.

6 | Stencil remaining tiles and let dry | Stencil rows of lettering across the three remaining tiles as you did in the previous step. Allow the paint to dry completely before proceeding. As you are waiting for the paint to dry, clean the texture paint off your stencil with a stencil cleaning brush. This is an important step, as texture paint will ruin the stencil if it is not removed immediately.

7 | Apply top layer of texture paint | Apply a thin layer of Cashmere texture paint on top of the stenciled lettering, smoothing it over the textured surface. Allow the paint to dry completely before proceeding.

8 | Prepare stenciling brush | Cut three or four paper towels into quarters, then layer the quarters into a single stack. Load a stenciling brush with Pine Green acrylic paint, then work the loaded brush in a circular motion onto the paper towel to remove the excess paint. This step is crucial to prevent paint from bleeding under the stencil.

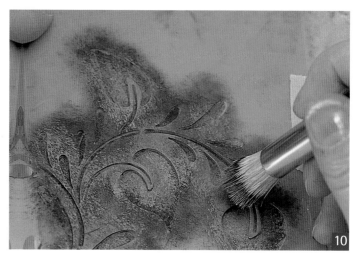

9 | **Stencil greenery** | Position the greenery stencil on the foam tile as desired and attach it with low-tack masking tape. Stipple stencil the Pine Green paint onto the surface, referring to the *Stenciling* instructions on pages 16–18 as needed. Apply the paint by pouncing the brush up and down onto the stencil openings, avoiding too heavy an application. Repeat with the three remaining tiles, varying the placement of the greenery design on each.

10 | **Add highlights to greenery** | Prepare the stenciling brush as you did in step 8 with Light Timberline Green acrylic paint. Reposition and secure the stencil over the existing greenery design on one tile. Using the same up-and-down pouncing motion, apply the paint to the surface over the stencil, adding highlights to the greenery. Repeat until you have highlighted all the greenery on each tile.

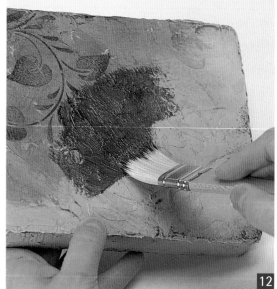

11 | **Allow stenciled design to dry** | Pull off the stencil to reveal the design beneath. Finish the three remaining tiles by stenciling highlights onto the greenery as desired. Allow the stenciled greenery to dry. While the paint is drying, clean the stencil.

12 | **Apply antiquing gel** | Brush antiquing gel onto a foam tile, covering an area no larger than 4" x 4" (10cm x 10cm) at a time before moving on to the next step.

tip

When completed, the four tiles will be displayed together as a single work of art. The tiles, therefore, function as parts of a whole. Before stenciling onto the tiles, consider how each tile will contribute to the overall design. You may want to stencil the words and/or the greenery so that they carry over from one tile to another. This unifies the components while adding some interest to the design. Before stenciling the tiles, it may help to map out a preliminary design on a sheet of scrap paper.

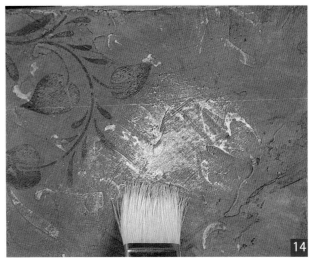

13 | Wipe off antiquing gel | Immediately after applying the antiquing gel to the foam tile, wipe a dry paper towel over the surface to remove excess gel. Use the same paint on-wipe off technique to cover the entire tile, including the edges. Repeat for the three remaining tiles.

14 | Apply gold highlights | Dab just the tip of a wide paintbrush into the Metallic Gold texture paint so the brush is mostly dry. Briskly run the brush back and forth across the surface, concentrating more paint toward the center. The gold paint should subtly highlight the underlayer of stenciled letters.

Cutting letter stencils apart sometimes makes stenciling easier. When you are working with individual letters, it is not always necessary to secure the stencil with tape; sometimes it is sufficient to hold it in place with your fingers while you apply the paint. Small-motif stencils fill in very quickly, so you rarely need to tape these stencils down. Just hold the stencil firmly to prevent it from slipping.

15 | Stencil letters and numbers | Position a letter or number stencil along the edge of one tile. Secure the stencil to the foam with low-tack masking tape, then mask off the flanking stencil openings with self-adhesive note paper. Stipple stencil the numbers and letters onto the foam tile with black acrylic paint as desired.

16 | **Finish stenciling** | Finish the other three tiles, using black paint to stipple stencil the rest of your design. Add interest by making one or more of the words carry over from one tile to another (see *Tip*, page 56).

17 | **Touch up** | With black acrylic paint and a fine paintbrush, touch up the letters and numbers by filling in the gaps left by the stencil bridges.

tip

If you wish, you can photocopy your photograph onto a sheet of Lazertran and apply it to the tile. The photocopied image will have a transparent background, allowing the surface of the tile to show through. Lazertran, a transfer decal paper, allows you to transfer your own color images onto almost any surface. You can purchase Lazertran at many craft and stamping supply stores.

18 | **Create sepia-toned image** | Photocopy a favorite family photograph on a color copier to get a sepia-toned image. This monochromatic sepia image will complement the ochres and browns of the tile designs.

19 | Adhere photograph to surface | Tear out the photocopy, ripping the paper away from you to avoid getting a white deckled edge. Brush the back of the paper with découpage medium, then place the picture on the design as desired. Apply a finishing coat of découpage medium over the picture to secure it to the foam tile. Burnish the picture with your finger to eliminate any bubbles. Allow the medium to dry.

The Finished Look

Displayed in an entranceway or your favorite room, these wall tiles accent your home while celebrating the family. Why not make a set of tiles as a gift for a close friend? Simply alter the elements and incorporate a favorite saying into the design.

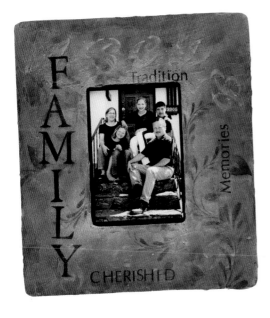

Variation: picture frame

This charming frame was made using the same techniques and paint colors on a wooden frame. If you have a particular photograph in mind for the frame, you can tailor the design and the lettering for a perfect match.

The perfect accent for any child's bathroom, this playful mirror makes washing up a fun task!

Good Clean Fun!
faux etched mirror

Offering a gentle reminder to scrub well, cheerful words of encouragement frame your young ones' faces as they gaze at their reflection. The letters, stenciled onto a mirror to resemble an etched surface, are sure to make cleaning fun. To create the frosted words, I used stencils for the "positive" letters and stickers for the "negative" letters. These simple lettering tools are both inexpensive and accessible, available in the scrapbook section of your local craft store.

TECHNIQUES USED IN THIS PROJECT
Applying a Basecoat (page 20)
Stenciling (pages 16–18)

MATERIALS AND TOOLS

wooden frame, with 12" x 12" (30cm x 30cm) opening

two 12" x 12" (30cm x 30cm) glass mirror tiles

Delta Ceramcoat acrylic paint
- White

Delta PermEnamel acrylic enamel paint
- Clear
- White

surface conditioner for mirror (rubbing alcohol or other conditioner; check instructions on packaging of acrylic enamel paints)

basecoating brush

dense foam stencil sponges or makeup sponges

alphabet stencils in six different letter styles, with 1" (3cm) high letters {BY PROVO CRAFT}

repositionable alphabet stickers, any style and color, with 1" (3cm) high letters {ALPHABIGGIES BY PROVO CRAFT}

100-grit sandpaper

plain white paper

metal ruler

pencil

scissors

black permanent marker

glass cutter, well oiled

palette

palette knife

cotton swabs

pins

liquid permanent adhesive

backing piece or 12" x 12" (30cm x 30cm) board

hammer and nails (or framer's point gun and points)

hanging hardware

safety gloves

safety goggles

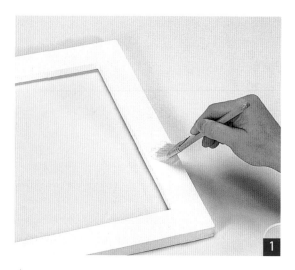

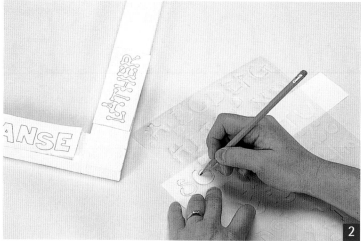

1 | Basecoat frame | Basecoat the wooden frame with white acrylic paint, sanding between each application of paint, as directed in the *Applying a Basecoat* instructions on page 20.

2 | Plan design | Cut a few strips of paper as wide as the width of the frame face. Decide which words you want to place around the frame, then stencil the words in pencil onto the strips of paper. You can use different stencils for different words. Cut the paper to divide each word into a single strip, then place the strips on the frame face. Complete enough words to cover the entire front surface of the frame.

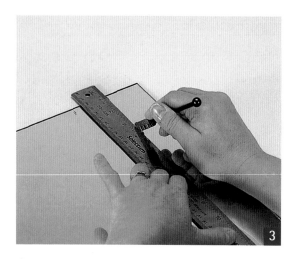

3 | Score mirror | Use a metal ruler and black permanent marker to measure and mark strips on the mirror that are equal to the width of the frame face. First, measure and make corresponding marks along the top and bottom edges of the mirror. Then, align the metal ruler with the top and bottom marks. Holding the ruler in place, run a well-oiled glass cutter along the edge of the ruler to score the mirror (see *Tip*, below).

4 | Break mirror | Wearing gloves and goggles, break the mirror along the score line by snapping it toward you.

tip

When working with glass, always wear gloves and safety goggles. To cut glass, you first need to create a score line (step 3, above). Hold the glass cutter at a 90° angle to the glass. With your free hand, hold a metal ruler in position on top of the glass. Using the ruler as your guide, start the glass cutter at the bottom edge of the glass and slide it forward, following the ruler all the way through to the top edge. A scratching sound indicates a good score line. After scoring the glass, *run* the glass by breaking it along the score line (step 4, at left). The score line causes a weakness in the glass that allows you to break it cleanly. A well-oiled glass cutter will produce smooth score lines, which will result in safe and easy breakage.

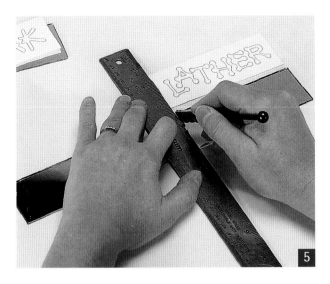

5 | **Cut mirror pieces** | Using the stenciled words from step 2 as a guide, cut the mirror strips into pieces that correspond to the paper pieces. When cutting the mirror strips, don't worry about trimming the ends perfectly straight, as cutting the ends at a slight angle will give the frame a more whimsical look. Keep all the left-over mirror pieces for later use.

6 | **Sand edges of all mirror pieces** | Wearing safety gloves, sand the edges of all the mirror pieces—even the scraps—using 100-grit sandpaper.

7 | **Condition mirror surface** | Condition the mirror surface, closely following the manufacturer's instructions on the label of the acrylic enamel paint. For most acrylic enamel paints or acrylic paints made for glass, the surface can be conditioned by cleaning it with rubbing alcohol.

8 | **Mix glaze and begin stenciling** | Make a faux glass-etching glaze by mixing one part white acrylic enamel paint with one part clear acrylic enamel paint. Mix the glaze with a palette knife on a palette. Add more white if you want your glaze to be frostier and more clear if you want it more transparent. Place the stencil as desired on a mirror strip, using the stenciled paper as a guide. Apply the paint, referring to the *Stenciling* instructions on pages 16–18 as needed. For a more whimsical look, bounce the letters. You should be able to complete an entire word with a sponge loaded only once. Stencil as many words as necessary to cover half the frame face.

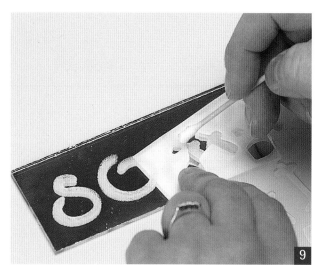

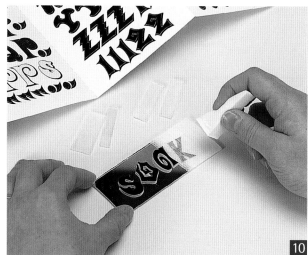

9 | **Remove interior openings** | For letters with interior openings, such as the letter *A*, remove the paint over the opening with a cotton swab while the paint is still wet. Some stencils include letter openings through which you can swab off the paint; otherwise, you can remove the paint freehand. Allow the paint to dry.

10 | **Create a "negative stencil"** | Again using the stenciled paper from step 2 as a guide, spell out words on the mirror strips, this time using self-adhesive letter stickers. Attach the stickers to the mirror strip, then apply the glaze over the adhered letters, using the stickers as a "negative stencil." Cover the exposed surface of the mirror strip evenly with glaze. Coat some of the scrap mirror pieces with glaze as well.

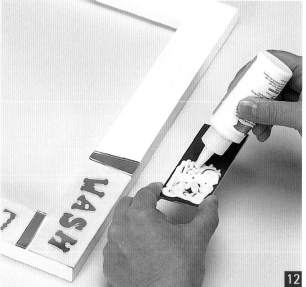

11 | **Remove stickers** | To remove the letter stickers, use a pin to lift each letter from the mirror surface while the paint is still wet. (The letters are reusable until they lose their stickiness.) Allow the paint to dry.

12 | **Glue mirror pieces to frame** | Lay the stenciled mirror pieces on the frame face, alternating the positive-stenciled words and the negative-stenciled words as desired. Leave spaces between each piece, then use the mirror scraps to fill these spaces until the entire frame face is covered. Use permanent adhesive to attach each piece to the frame surface.

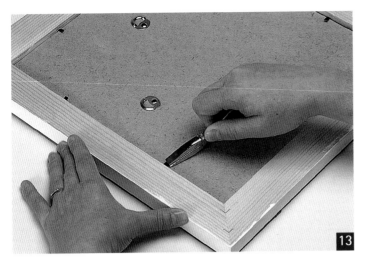

13 | **Secure mirror in frame** | Secure the mirror in the frame. If the frame comes with a backing piece, secure it with the built-in hardware. If it doesn't come with a backing, cut a 12" x 12" (30cm x 30cm) board, place it behind the mirror, then carefully secure both pieces inside the frame with nails or framing points. Add hanging hardware as necessary.

IN OTHER WORDS

Use your choice of words, phrases and sayings to embellish the *Good Clean Fun! Faux Etched Mirror.* Looking for a little inspiration? Here are some ideas you may find helpful:

- Cleanse
- Soak
- Scrub
- Lather
- Dry
- Wash
- Repeat

The Finished Look

With lively lettering in a variety of font styles, this mirror is a fun way to remind the kids to wash!

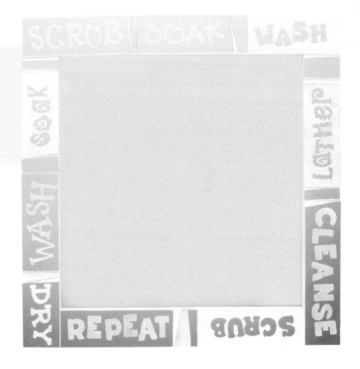

Variation: apothecary jars

Now that you have the stencils, use the same positive- and negative-stenciling techniques to decorate matching containers. You can also use a white paint pen to add handwritten words in casual, cursive script. To give a glass jar a mirror effect, spray paint the inside of it silver.

A combination of floral patterns and flourished lettering gives this découpaged box a vintage, romantic look.

$\mathcal{R}$omantic monogrammed box

Combine soft-hued decorative paper with a variety of letter and image stickers to create this keepsake box. Or, for a more personal touch, use color copies of old letters or other ephemera in place of the decorative paper. This beautiful box is made to accessorize a woman's boudoir. With its heirloom quality, it would make a wonderful birthday or bridal shower gift.

MATERIALS AND TOOLS

wooden box with hinged top, 5" x 6½" x 3"
(13cm x 17cm x 8cm)

Delta Ceramcoat acrylic paint
- Light Ivory

satin découpage medium

brushes
- basecoating brush
- sponge brush

stickers {BY K&COMPANY}
- English florals and vines
- borders, corners and journal tags
- floral alphabet

dimensional resin stickers
- alphabet {LIFE'S JOURNEY DOMED GOUDY ALPHABET
  BY K&COMPANY}
- large square Page Pebbles

decorative paper {BY K&COMPANY}
- English floral accents
- handwritten letters

screwdriver

100-grit sandpaper

sliding paper trimmer (or a craft knife, metal ruler and cutting pad)

liquid permanent adhesive

OPTIONAL: small three-dimensional charms and wire cutters

OPTIONAL: gold box latch and clasp, ruler and pencil

TECHNIQUES USED IN THIS PROJECT

Applying a Basecoat (page 20)
Découpaging (page 22)

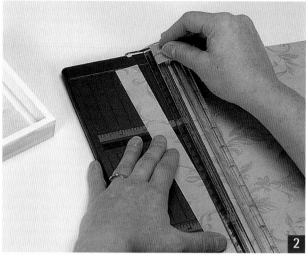

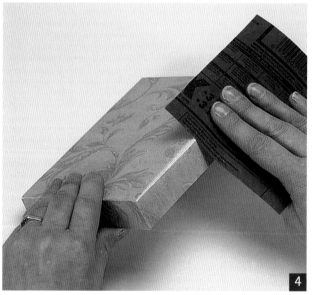

1 I **Basecoat box interior** I Using a screwdriver, remove the box hinges and set them aside. Basecoat the interior of the box and lid with Light Ivory acrylic paint, sanding between each application, as directed in the *Applying a Basecoat* instructions on page 20. You do not have to completely cover the top and bottom surfaces, but make sure to paint all the edges and work the paint into every corner, as shown. Allow the paint to dry.

2 I **Cut paper to size** I With a sliding paper trimmer, cut the decorative paper to the size of each exterior box side to be covered. If you don't have a paper trimmer, you can use a craft knife, a metal ruler and a cutting pad.

3 I **Cover box with paper** I Brush découpage medium onto the back of the trimmed paper, then adhere each piece to the appropriate side of the box. After adhering the paper, smooth out any bubbles with your fingers.

4 I **Sand edges** I Using 100-grit sandpaper, sand the edges of the box to shear off any irregular areas. When sanding, hold the sandpaper at a 45° angle to the edge, as shown; this will prevent you from sanding away the decorative paper. Continue until all the edges are even and the lid meets flush with the base.

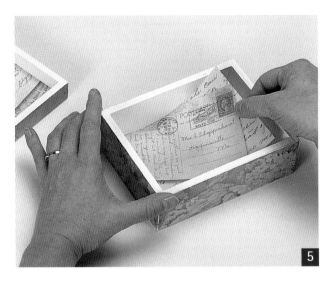

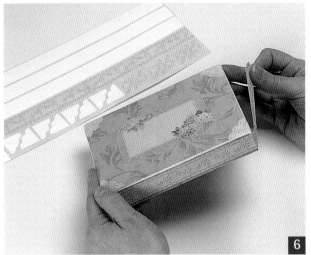

5 | **Line lid and base** | Measure and cut the decorative paper to fit the interior of the box lid and base. I chose paper that has the look of handwritten letters and envelopes, but you can use copies of your own letters to line the inside of the box. For a perfect fit, trim the paper just slightly smaller than the actual box dimensions. Apply découpage medium to the back of the paper, then adhere it to the wooden surface. Eliminate any bubbles by smoothing out the paper with your fingers.

6 | **Create first design layer and border** | Gather all the materials to be used for the box's exterior design, including decorative paper and self-adhesive stickers. Compose your découpage design by arranging the materials as desired on the box lid. Attach the first layer of elements: a base of the largest components on the top of the lid, followed by a border along the edges of the lid.

7 | **Complete découpage design** | Add the final layers of elements, lifting, tucking, overlapping and running any materials over the edge as desired. Include your monogram, initials and any other lettering that you have selected. Do not be afraid to cut stickers and images to fit the design.

Monograms serve as your own personal logo and as a sign of pride in your family name. A formal monogram consists of the initials of your birth name. This includes the formal version of your first name (*Robert* rather than *Bob*, for example) and middle name, as infrequently as you may use either of these. There are never more than three initials in a monogram, even if you are blessed with many names.

The order of the initials is dictated by the style of the monogram. When letters are the same size, the monogram reads in the following order: first initial, middle initial, last initial. For married women, a formal monogram reads: first initial, maiden surname initial, married surname initial. When the monogram style includes a larger center letter, the monogram reads in the following order: first initial, last initial, middle initial; or, for married women: first initial, married surname initial, maiden surname initial. For surnames that begin with *Mc*, both characters are used but take up the space of only one.

Monograms with three initials are the most common, but single and double initial monograms are also acceptable. Virkotype monograms are shaped like an oval and framed. When additional motifs and decorations are added to a monogram of any kind, it becomes a logo.

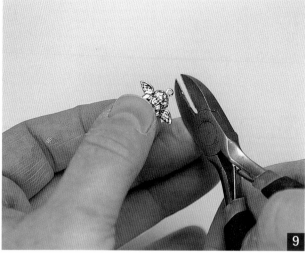

8 | **Coat box with découpage medium** | Once your découpage arrangement is complete and you are pleased with the design, use your hand to burnish all the materials flat to the box surface. Brush a coat of découpage medium onto the exterior surface of the box. Allow the medium to dry, then add a second coat.

9 | **Prepare additional materials** | If you are adding charms or other small three-dimensional objects to the surface design, remove any hangers, findings or extraneous attachments with wire cutters.

10 | **Add dimensional objects** | After the second coat of découpage medium has dried, attach the final elements, including the dimensional resin stickers. (Do not varnish over these stickers or they will lose their clear, dimensional quality.) Use permanent adhesive to attach charms or other small objects to the surface.

11 | **Decorate lid interior** | Flip the lid over, then découpage the interior surface as desired. Add elements to create an arrangement that echoes the exterior design.

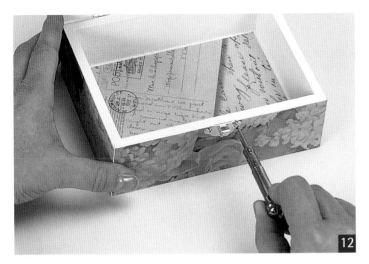

12 | Reattach hinges | Use the screwdriver to reattach the hinges that you removed in step 1. If you want to add a latch to the box, first mark the center of the box with a ruler and pencil, then attach the latch at the center.

The Finished Look

With its soft, feminine look, this monogrammed box functions wonderfully as a jewelry box. It is perfect for anybody that has a taste for vintage Victorian style.

Variation: dresser tray

You can create a dresser set with this oval tray, découpaged to match the box. Give the tray its own distinct look by adding torn pieces of decorative paper along the rim.

I enjoy livening up my lettered projects with words and expressions in other languages.

Italian bread basket tray

Lettering your projects in another language can be a great way to honor your heritage, celebrate a favorite culture or just add a touch of elegance to your table. Because Italy is often associated with delicious food, I chose an Italian theme for this bread basket tray. To evoke the look of hand-painted Italian ceramics, I used an Italian saying, an olive-branch motif and an informal brush-lettering style. You can draw from the culture of other Mediterranean areas, such as Greece or Provence, for a slightly different style or a new saying.

MATERIALS AND TOOLS

rectangular woven bread basket, 12" x 17" x 3" (30cm x 43cm x 8cm), with 10" x 15½" (25cm x 39cm) removable wooden tray

photocopy of *Bread Basket Design Template*, enlarged as directed, page 120

Casual Italian Alphabet Guide, page 121

Delta Ceramcoat acrylic paint
  - Burnt Umber
  - Chocolate Cherry
  - Light Timberline Green
  - Payne's Gray
  - Pine Green
  - Timberline Green
  - Trail Tan

acrylic gel stain medium

acrylic matte spray varnish

acrylic thinner

satin acrylic varnish

brushes
  - brushes for basecoating and varnishing
  - round brushes (no. 3, no. 6)
  - filbert brushes (no. 4, no. 8)

stencil sponge

stencils
  - small diamond border stencil {BY PLAID ENTERPRISES, INC.}
  - diamond background stencil {HARLEQUIN BY DELTA}

soft cloth

100-grit sandpaper

low-tack masking tape

tracing paper

water-erasable transfer paper

ballpoint pen

paper towels

OPTIONAL: embossing stylus

TECHNIQUES USED IN THIS PROJECT
Applying a Basecoat (page 20)
Stenciling (pages 16–18)
Brush Lettering (page 13)

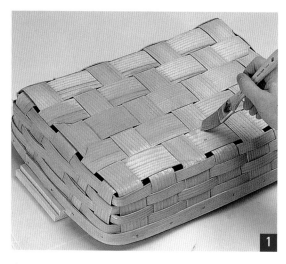

1 | Apply undercoat to basket | Prepare an undercoat glaze by mixing Light Timberline Green acrylic paint with an equal amount of acrylic gel stain medium. Brush a light coat of the glaze onto the basket so that the wood grain is still visible. Paint both handles with Trail Tan acrylic paint. Allow the glaze and paint to dry.

2 | Apply stain to basket | Prepare a stain by mixing Burnt Umber acrylic paint with an equal amount of acrylic gel stain medium. With a wide paintbrush, apply the stain to the basket, working it into the entire surface, including all crevices. Cover only a small section, about 6" (15cm) square, before moving on to step 3.

3 | Remove excess stain | After applying stain to a section of the basket, wipe the excess stain off with a soft cloth. (You can also use a paper towel but you will have to replace it often with new pieces.) As you work, rotate the basket and check for unpainted spots; reach the bristles of your brush into these areas to apply the stain. Working in 6" (15cm) square sections at a time, repeat steps 2 and 3 until the entire basket is covered. Allow the stain to dry.

4 | Spray with matte finish | When the basket is completely dry, spray two coats of matte finish over the entire surface in a well-ventilated area.

5 | Basecoat tray | Basecoat the wooden tray with Trail Tan acrylic paint, sanding between each application of paint, as directed in the *Applying a Basecoat* instructions on page 20. Allow the paint to dry.

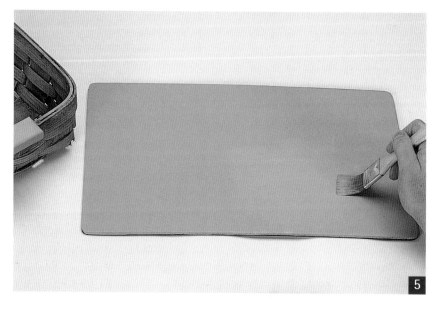

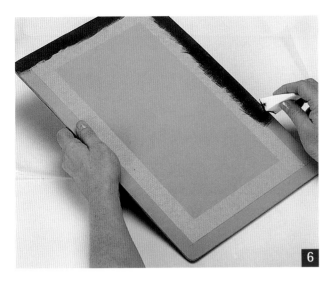

6 | **Paint border** | Use low-tack masking tape to mask off a ¾" (19mm) border around the perimeter of the tray. Apply a single coat of Chocolate Cherry acrylic paint to the masked-off border area and tray edges with a stencil sponge, pouncing the loaded sponge up and down on the surface. Do not make the application too dense; allow some of the background color to show through. Allow the paint to dry.

7 | **Stencil border design** | Attach the small diamond stencil over the border section, using low-tack masking tape to keep it in position. Apply Light Timberline Green acrylic paint over the stencil with a stencil sponge, referring to the *Stenciling* instructions on pages 16–18 as needed. When the entire border is complete, remove the stencil and use the tip of a round paintbrush to add a dot of Payne's Gray acrylic paint between every diamond. Allow the paint to dry.

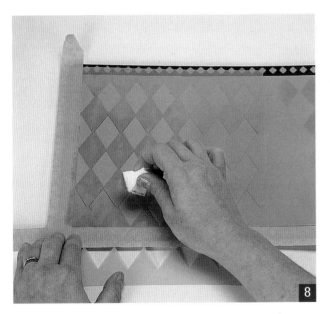

8 | **Stencil background design** | Attach the large diamond stencil to the tray with low-tack masking tape, positioning the tape so it masks off the border. Mix a few drops of Chocolate Cherry with Trail Tan to create a muddy-khaki color. Use this mixture to stencil the diamonds onto the tray. Continue stenciling from the top right toward the center until there is no more paint on the sponge. Repeat with the lower left area. Leave the upper left, bottom right and center unpainted.

9 | **Transfer pattern onto tray** | Place a piece of tracing paper over the photocopied pattern, then trace the pattern with a pen. Position a piece of transfer paper on the tray, with the waxy side facing the tray surface, then place the traced pattern on top. Hinge the traced pattern and transfer paper to the tray with low-tack masking tape along the top. Using an embossing stylus or ballpoint pen, trace over a few lines of the pattern. Lift the paper and check the tray to make sure the transfer was successful. If so, continue tracing until the entire design is transferred to the tray.

10 | Paint letters | Paint the letters with Payne's Gray, using a no. 4 filbert brush for the smaller letters and a no. 8 filbert for the larger ones. The width of the brush should equal the width of the letters so that you can complete the lettering with single, smooth strokes rather than "painting in" the lines. A round brush can be used instead, but the filbert's rounded tip is more effective in producing clean, rounded ends on the letters.

11 | Paint main leaves | Load a no. 6 round brush with Timberline Green, then dab the end of the brush into Pine Green. Paint all the leaves except those that are dotted. As you apply the paint, allow the two colors on the brush to blend on the tray surface. If you do not get the effect of double colors, load the brush with only one color at a time, applying Timberline Green first, followed by Pine Green. Touch up with a second application if necessary.

12 | Paint olives | Using the filbert brushes, paint in the form of the olives with Chocolate Cherry. Shade the olives with Payne's Gray and highlight with Light Timberlake Green.

13 | Paint olive branch | Mix Chocolate Cherry into Pine Green until you get a dark green. Paint the olive branch and the veins of the leaves using this mixture and a no. 3 round paintbrush.

14 | Paint remaining leaves | Mix equal parts of Light Timberlake Green and acrylic thinner with a touch of Chocolate Cherry to get an olive-colored wash. Brush on the wash to define the remaining leaves (outlined with dotted lines). To create the shape of the leaf, touch the fine point of a loaded round brush against the surface. Press the brush down as you move it across the surface for a thicker line, then return to the fine point as you finish the leaf. Because it is a light wash, you can brush it over other painted areas on the surface.

15 | Varnish tray | When all the paint is completely dry, gently pass a damp paper towel over the tray to erase the lines left by the transfer paper. Allow the tray to dry completely, making sure the surface is no longer damp from the paper towel. Brush on three coats of satin varnish, letting the varnish dry between each coat.

IN OTHER WORDS

Use your choice of words, phrases and sayings to embellish the *Italian Bread Basket Tray*. Looking for a little inspiration? Here are some ideas you may find helpful:

- *Canta che ti passa.*
  (Sing and it will pass.)
- *A tavola non si invecchia mai.*
  (You never age at the dinner table.)
- *Benvenuti in questa casa.*
  (Welcome to this house.)
- *Amici e vino devono essere vecchi.* (Friends and wine must be old.)

The Finished Look

If your basket has a removable wooden bottom, you can paint a second design on the opposite side. Whether you display it on a shelf, hang it on a wall or use it to serve bread, the finished tray warms up any kitchen.

Variation: welcome sign

Featuring casual lettering and the olive branch motif, this small wooden plaque greets visitors with the Italian expression for "Welcome to this house."

Stenciled with a child's monogram, the alphabet and a moon-and-stars design, this charming memory box is a treasure.

Baby memory box

This sweet baby memory box is ideal for storing precious memorabilia from the baby's first year, such as a hospital bracelet, a little knitted hat, photographs, a first spoon or a rattle. If you are making the box for a baby shower and the baby's name has not been chosen yet, substitute *ABC* for the monogram. This is one gift that is sure to be cherished for years to come!

MATERIALS AND TOOLS

oval bentwood box, 6½" x 8½" x 3½" (17cm x 22cm x 9cm)

photocopy of *Moon and Stars Template*, enlarged as directed, page 121

photocopy of *Block Letter Alphabet Template*, enlarged as directed, page 122

Delta Ceramcoat acrylic paint
- Blueberry
- Chambray Blue
- Metallic Gold
- Purple Dusk

acrylic spray sealer

satin acrylic varnish

brushes
- brushes for basecoating and varnishing
- disposable glue brush

dense foam roller

stencil sponge

dark blue suede paper, plain and embossed

100-grit sandpaper

tracing paper

black permanent pen

low-tack masking tape

freezer paper

self-healing cutting mat

round-handled craft knife with sharp no. 11 blade

palette (or baking parchment paper taped to table)

paint spatula

fine-point metallic paint markers, gold and silver

white glue

spray adhesive (or low-tack masking tape; see *Making Your Own Stencils*, page 80)

TECHNIQUES USED IN THIS PROJECT
Applying a Basecoat (page 20)
Stenciling (pages 16–18)
Hand Lettering (page 12)

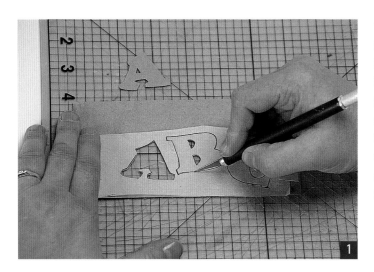

1 | **Cut stencils** | Place a sheet of tracing paper over the photocopy of the alphabet template, then trace the letters with a black permanent pen. Cut sheets of freezer paper into strips as wide as the height of the box. Use low-tack masking tape to attach the lettering patterns to the waxy side of the freezer paper strips. Then, place the strips of paper on a cutting mat; do not tape the papers to the mat. Use a craft knife with a no. 11 blade to cut your own alphabet stencils from the freezer paper, penetrating through both the tracing paper and the freezer paper for a clean cut. When cutting letters with interior spaces, cut the interior space first, then cut out the letter. Reserve the cut-out letters for later use.

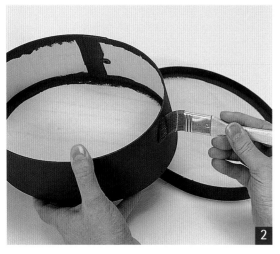

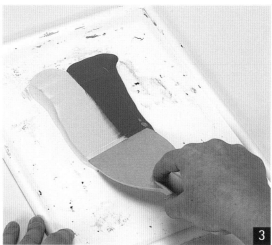

2 | **Basecoat wooden box** | Basecoat the wooden box with Blueberry acrylic paint, sanding between each application, as directed in the *Applying a Basecoat* instructions on page 20. You do not have to cover the entire interior, but do apply paint to the crevices and corners inside the box, as shown.

3 | **Prepare palette** | Pour puddles of Purple Dusk and Chambray Blue acrylic paints next to each other on a palette. Use a paint spatula to pull the paint down in parallel bands.

• Making Your Own Stencils •

It's easier than you may think to cut your own stencils. Follow these few tips for stencil-making:

~ Using freezer paper as the stencil material makes cutting quick and effortless. Freezer paper is available in both white and kraft (brown) colors. Traditionally, it is coated with wax on one side, but nowadays most freezer paper has a plastic coating instead. I recommend using freezer paper with a plastic coating, not wax, for the best results.

~ Before cutting, secure the pattern to the freezer paper with low-tack masking tape, but do not tape the papers to the cutting mat. This allows you to move the paper around so that you are always cutting toward you.

~ After each letter is cut out, remove it to make sure that you have applied enough pressure with the blade to make a clean cut.

~ Once cut, coat the back of the stencil (the non-shiny side) with a spray adhesive and let it dry before placing it on your surface. Drying makes the adhesive repositionable. You can also adhere the stencil to the surface with low-tack masking tape. Do not wash the stencils after use, as they will disintegrate. Between uses, place the stencils on sheets of freezer paper and store flat.

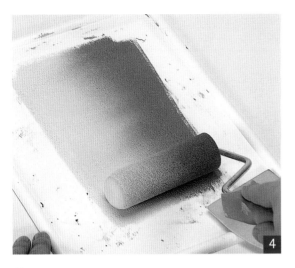

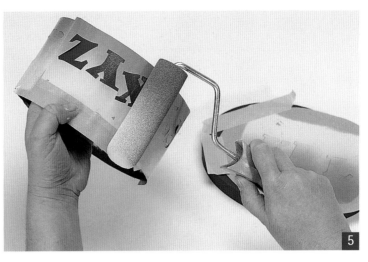

4 | **Load roller with paint** | Run the dense foam roller through the paint, blending the two colors as you load the roller. Continue until there is a gradation of one color into the next rather than two separate lines of color.

5 | **Stencil letters** | Wrap the stencil strips made in step 1 around the entire box, then secure them to the side of the box with low-tack masking tape. Roll the dense foam roller loaded with paint over the stencil, applying consistent pressure to produce an even coat. Stencil a monogram on the box lid in the same manner. When you are finished, remove the stencils and allow the paint to dry. Do not worry if the paint bleeds under the stencil openings; you will be able to conceal this when outlining the letters in step 8.

Note: After painting, put the roller directly in a sealable plastic bag or right into water; otherwise, the paint will dry quickly on the roller.

6 | **Finish letters** | Take the letters that you reserved in step 1 and select the letters that have interior spaces, such as *A*, *B* and *D*. Align these letters directly on top of the stenciled letters and secure each letter to the box with low-tack masking tape. Load a stencil sponge with Blueberry paint, then pounce the loaded sponge up and down onto the box to fill in the letters' interior spaces.

7 | **Stencil moon and stars** | Place a sheet of tracing paper over the photocopy of the *Moon and Stars* template, then trace the design with a black permanent pen. Using this tracing paper as a guide, create a stencil for the moon and stars out of freezer paper as you did for the alphabet in step 1. Position the moon stencil as desired on the box lid, then stencil the design onto the surface with Metallic Gold acrylic paint and a stencil sponge. To make the gold paint show up against the dark blue surface, stencil on one coat of paint, let dry, then apply another coat. Stencil the stars onto the lid and around the sides of the box, this time applying only one coat of paint.

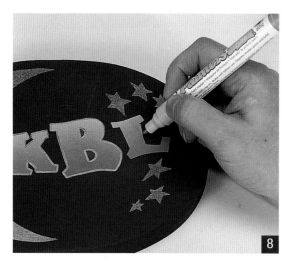

8 | **Outline stenciled letters** | Outline each of the stenciled letters with a gold paint pen (see *Tip*, below). If necessary, you can use the outlining to conceal any imperfect edges.

tip

When working with a new paint pen, you need to prime the pen to start the flow of paint to the nib. With the cap on, shake the pen well. As you shake, you should be able to hear the movement of the mixing ball inside. Start the paint flow by gently depressing the tip of the marker, holding it on a paper surface until you see the paint flow into the tip. This can take 10 to 60 seconds. Repeat as necessary during use. To prolong the life of the pen, keep it tightly capped when not in use.

9 | **Add stardust** | With a silver paint pen, add decorative stars and stardust to the letters along the side of the box. If desired, handwrite any text, such as a child's name or a saying, around the sides of the box with the same paint pen. If you're nervous about lettering freehand, sketch it out first with a chalk pencil.

10 | **Seal and varnish** | When the paint is completely dry, spray the box and box lid with acrylic sealer. Let the sealer dry, then brush on two coats of satin varnish.

Baby Boxes for Charity

I was inspired to create this project by The Memory Box Artist Program, the brainchild of artist Tera Leigh. This volunteer program provides hand-decorated boxes for families of infants that pass away in the hospital. In their time of grief, families are given a beautiful box, lovingly made by an artist, so they do not have to leave the hospital without any record of their child's life. To date, the program has provided 60,000 boxes to infant bereavement programs free of charge. If you enjoyed making this project, you might consider sharing your talent to make a box for this worthwhile charity. For more information on The Memory Box Artist Program, go to www.memoryboxes.org.

11 | Line box interior | With a craft knife and a cutting mat, cut the suede paper into pieces to fit on the interior bottom, on the interior lid and around the interior sides. Brush white glue onto the back of the suede paper, then press the paper to the wood surface. As you are fitting and adhering the paper, avoid getting glue on the box exterior.

The Finished Look

This painted box is designed to hold mementos from your baby's first years. If the memory box is for an older child or a teenager, simply change the look to fit his or her personality!

Variation: memory album

For those photographs and cards that document the baby's first year, create a wooden memory album to complement the box. An additional stencil was cut to add the child's first name to the front of the album. This finished album holds 8½" x 11" (22cm x 28cm) memory sheets.

Add a touch of inspiration to your work space with this Bulletin Board, which features several lettering techniques.

Create! bulletin board

To embellish this project, I included stamped polymer clay tags, stenciling, hand lettering and premade scrapbooking accents. You, however, are not limited to these design options; since creativity is the theme of this project, feel free to choose the lettering techniques that you enjoy the most. Though single words were used on this bulletin board, you might also consider adding particular quotes or sayings that you find especially inspirational. And, the theme can always be changed to fit the environment. The creativity theme works well in a crafter's studio, but something different, such as a sports theme, might work well in a child's bedroom.

TECHNIQUES USED IN THIS PROJECT
Working with Polymer Clay (page 21)
Stamping on Polymer Clay (page 15)
Applying a Basecoat (page 20)
Stenciling (pages 16–18)
Hand Lettering (page 12)

MATERIALS AND TOOLS

octagonal wooden frame, 17³/₄" (45cm) diameter with 12" x 12" (30cm x 30cm) opening

Delta Ceramcoat acrylic paint
- Aquamarine
- Blue Lagoon
- Caribbean Blue
- Lime Green
- Metallic Silver

acrylic gel stain medium

acrylic spray sealer

light blue polymer clay, conditioned

polymer clay tools
- ceramic tile
- acrylic rod
- craft knife
- oven

brushes
- basecoating brush
- 1" (3cm)-wide wash brush with soft goat hair bristles

stencil sponges

rubber stamps {BY PSX}
- basic lettering, lowercase and uppercase

alphabet stencil with 1" (3cm) letters {UPPERCASE LETTERS BY PLAID ENTERPRISES, INC.}

1½" (4cm) wooden letters

laser-cut metal words

polymer clay tag templates

small screw(s)

silver metallic paste {RUB 'N BUFF}

double-sided tape

waxed paper

100-grit sandpaper

medium-tip metallic silver paint pen

liquid permanent adhesive

12" x 12" (30cm x 30cm) corkboard and 12" x 12" (30cm x 30cm) cardboard (or backing piece)

hammer and nails (or framer's point gun and points)

hanging hardware

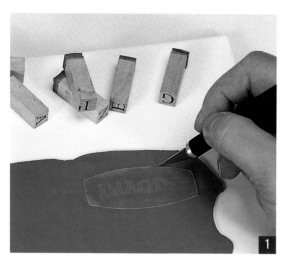

1 | **Make clay tags** | On a ceramic tile, roll out the conditioned polymer clay to a sheet 3/32" (2mm) thick. Using small alphabet letter stamps, stamp words on the clay sheet. Center and position a template over the clay to frame each word, then cut around the template using a craft knife, as shown. Impress the top of a small screw onto each corner for a decorative effect.

2 | **Bake and gild clay tags** | Bake the clay tags at 275°F (135°C) for 20 minutes, then let tags cool. Dab a bit of silver metallic paste on your finger. Rub the paste over the surface of the tags to highlight the top of the design.

3 | **Paint wood letters** | Apply a strip of double-sided tape to a piece of waxed paper. Place the wood letters on top of the tape to keep them in place. Paint the letters with Blue Lagoon acrylic paint. When dry, apply silver metallic paste to the tops of the letters only, allowing some of the blue to show through.

4 | **Paint frame** | Basecoat the entire frame with Caribbean Blue acrylic paint, sanding between each layer, as directed in the *Applying a Basecoat* instructions on page 20. Prepare three color glazes by mixing equal parts of gel stain medium with the Aquamarine, Blue Lagoon and Lime Green acrylic paints. With a soft brush, apply patches of each glaze to the frame surface. Brush the colors together so no harsh lines show; using the brush without rinsing between colors will allow them to gently blend.

5 | **Add first layer of words** | When you are satisfied with the finish of the frame, allow the paint to dry. Stencil words onto the frame with a stencil sponge and Metallic Silver acrylic paint, following the *Stenciling* guidelines on pages 16–18. After the stenciling is complete, fill in any bridges with paint to give the letters a less stenciled look. Next, use a silver metallic paint pen to handwrite words onto the frame. Allow the paint to dry, then coat the entire surface of the frame with spray sealer.

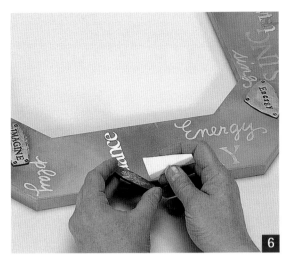

6 | **Finish with additional elements** | Arrange the polymer clay tags, the wooden letters and the laser-cut metal words on the frame, orienting them in different directions to add interest. Dab a small amount of permanent adhesive on the back of each element, then press it onto the surface as desired. Place a sheet of waxed paper followed by a heavy weight onto the metal words to make them bond flush with the frame.

7 | **Insert corkboard** | Insert corkboard, cut to size, into the back of the frame. Place a piece of cardboard cut to the same size behind the corkboard and secure it in the frame with nails or framer's points. Add hanging hardware.

The Finished Look

To accessorize your bulletin board, create lettered thumb-tacks. Simply stamp individual letters on card stock, then use hot glue to attach the flat side of a clear marble nugget to the top of each letter. Trim the excess paper and glue the marbles to the tops of the thumbtacks.

Variation: polymer clay tags

The polymer clay tags made in step 1 are great accents for cards and scrapbook pages. Clay gift tags can also be made by using tag templates and a plastic straw for the hole. After baking and gilding the tags, loop decorative cords, ribbons or embellishments through the holes.

Wake up to this lively canister, designed to hold your coffee beans and perk up your kitchen décor.

Caffeine canister

Rubber stamps, polymer clay and powdered pigments turn an ordinary stainless steel canister into a one-of-a-kind accent piece. To reflect the caffeine theme, the canister is embellished with fun lettering and funky metallic tiles. By bouncing the letters as you stamp, you not only add to the playful energy of the design, you alleviate the concern of having to keep the letters perfectly straight.

MATERIALS AND TOOLS

stainless steel canister
(NOTE: Make sure your canister, including the lid, is oven-safe by testing it in the oven first.)

brushes
- soft paintbrushes (any size)
- disposable glue brush

brown polymer clay, conditioned

polymer clay tools
- ceramic tile
- acrylic rod
- craft knife
- oven

rubber stamps
- small whimsical alphabet {BY HERO ARTS}
- set of four swirl patterns, each stamp 1" (3 cm) {BY QUATROS, HERO ARTS}

Staz-On black solvent ink pad

stamp cleaning pad

Staz-On stamp cleaner fluid for solvent ink

metal ruler

cornstarch powder

metallic powdered pigments
- antique copper
- gold
- silver
- russet

thin white glue

TECHNIQUES USED IN THIS PROJECT
Working with Polymer Clay (page 21)
Rubber Stamping (page 14)
Stamping on Polymer Clay (page 15)

1 | **Make clay tile sheets** | On a ceramic tile, roll out the conditioned polymer clay to a sheet about ⅛" (3mm) thick. Using a metal ruler, measure out and mark a grid on the sheet to create 1" (3cm) square tiles. Cut along the grid lines with a sharp craft knife to divide the sheet, but do not separate the tiles. Make about forty tiles, creating another sheet if necessary. Reserve a section of the clay sheet for step 6.

2 | **Stamp tile sheets** | Use a soft paintbrush to coat the surface of the sheet(s) with cornstarch powder. Working in vertical rows, impress one stamp into each square tile. Stamp the same design on all the tiles in two consecutive rows; change stamps for the next two rows, and so on.

3 | **Gild tile sheets** | Dip a soft paintbrush into one container of metallic powdered pigment, then lightly brush the pigment onto the tile squares. Keep the application light so that some of the brown polymer clay shows underneath the pigment. Gild all the tiles of one design the same metallic color, applying the powdered pigment to one vertical row at a time.

4 | **Apply tiles to canister** | Using a disposable glue brush, apply thin white glue to the canister where the tiles are going to be placed. Use the clay blade to lift the tiles and place them in rows around the canister, as shown. Trim the last tile as necessary to complete the row. Add another row of tiles.

5 | **Stamp letters and add tiles** | Following the *Rubber Stamping* guidelines on page 14, stamp letter by letter to add coffee-related words to the surface of the canister. Bounce the letters to avoid having to follow a straight line. Glue a tile between each word; if you come to a space where there is not enough room to stamp a word, add a few more tiles instead. To avoid smearing the ink, hold the canister from the inside. If you make a mistake or smear the ink, use stamp cleaner to immediately remove the ink, then restamp. Add a few tiles along the bottom edge of the canister.

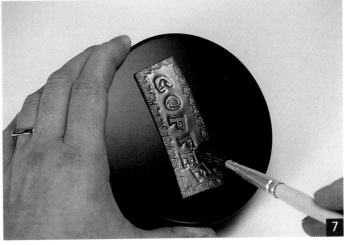

6 | Make label | Cut a 1" x 3" (3cm x 8cm) rectangle from the sheet of clay. Use alphabet stamps to stamp the word *coffee* in the rectangle, then use decorative stamps to add a border along the edges of the label. If any distortion occurs while stamping, trim the edges evenly with a sharp craft knife. Brush metallic powdered pigment onto the label, adding and blending a strip of each metallic color.

7 | Apply label and bake | Brush thin white glue onto the back of the clay label, then press it onto the center of the lid. With a soft brush, remove the excess powder. Bake the canister and the lid. If there are fingerprints on the stainless steel surface, wait until after the canister has been baked to wipe them off.

The Finished Look

Filled with coffee beans, this coffee canister, with its hip design and contemporary feel, is the perfect addition to a gourmet gift basket.

IN OTHER WORDS

Use your choice of words, phrases and sayings to embellish the *Caffeine Canister*. Looking for a little inspiration? Here are some ideas you may find helpful:

- Espresso
- Cappuccino
- Café Latte
- Café au Lait
- Machiatto
- Café Mocha
- Cafecito
- Mocha Latte
- Java

Variation: sugar and cocoa tins

Complete the set with matching sugar and cocoa canisters. Keep the stainless steel look, but add a little variety by using small, stackable tins.

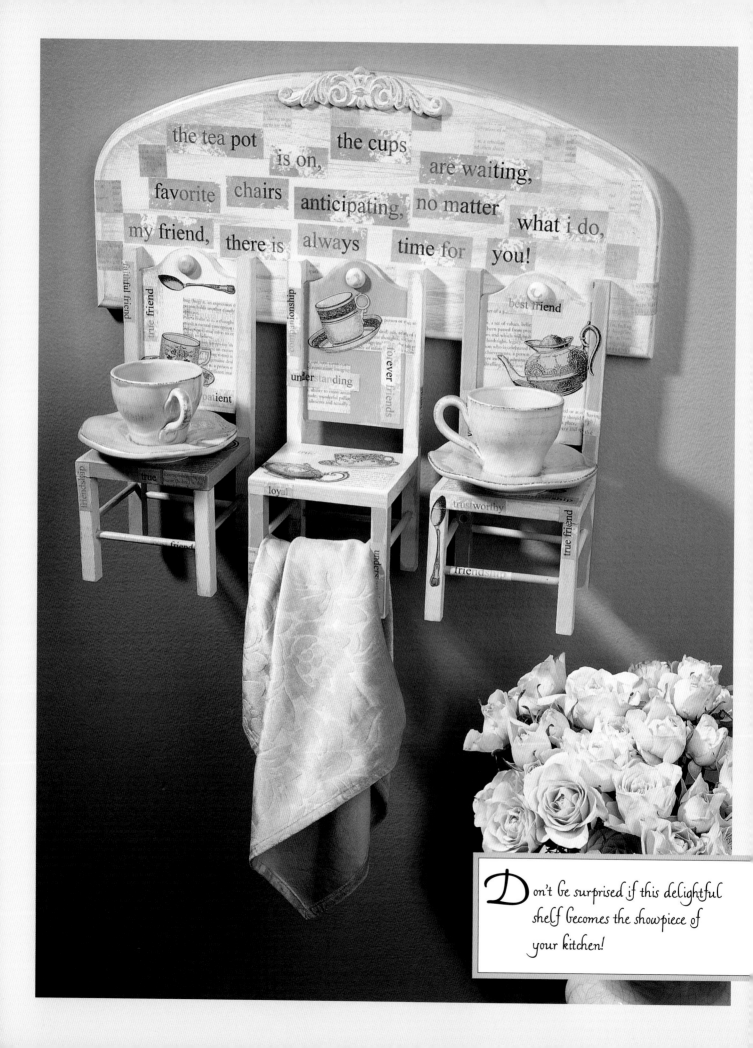

Don't be surprised if this delightful shelf becomes the showpiece of your kitchen!

Tea Time chair shelf

Usually when crafting a project, I look for a saying to fit the theme. In this case, however, I found the saying first, and it inspired me to make this quaint Chair Shelf.

The teapot is on, the cups are waiting,

favorite chairs anticipating.

No matter what I have to do,

my friend, there is always time for you.

The text for this poem was generated on the computer, antiqued, then découpaged onto the pegboard and chairs for a unique vintage look.

MATERIALS AND TOOLS

three wooden chairs, $4\frac{1}{2}$" x 10" x $4\frac{1}{2}$" (11cm x 25cm x 11cm) each

hat rack pegboard, with pegs removed; carved wooden accent and small wooden buttons or plugs for pegboard

computer (with Times New Roman or other desired font) and printer

photocopier

Delta Ceramcoat acrylic paint
- Antique White
- Cactus Green
- Hydrangea Pink
- Trail Tan

satin découpage medium

satin acrylic varnish

brushes
- brushes for basecoating and varnishing
- sponge brush

sea sponge

copyright-free vintage images of tea and coffee items, such as teacups, teapots, coffee cups and spoons

standard white computer paper

12" x 12" (30cm x 30cm) decorative paper with newspaper-like lettering {HOT OFF THE PRESS, INC.}

antiquing solution: $\frac{1}{4}$ cup (60ml) instant coffee granules mixed with 2 cups (474ml) hot water

waxed paper

craft knife

scissors

sliding paper trimmer

beeswax or white candle

100-grit sandpaper

ruler or measuring tape

pencil

hand drill and thick wooden board for drilling surface

screwdriver and three 1" (3cm) woodscrews

white glue

hammer and small finishing nails

TECHNIQUES USED IN THIS PROJECT

Using a Computer to Generate Lettering (pages 10–11)

Antiquing Paper (page 23)

Découpaging (page 22)

1 | Copy and antique images | Make several photocopies of vintage tea- and coffee-related images, then lay out the copies on top of waxed paper sheets. Antique the images, following the *Antiquing Paper* guidelines on page 23. Brush the coffee solution over the images, allowing puddles to form on the paper. Allow the paper to dry completely.

2 | Print and antique words | Use a computer and printer to generate tea- and friendship-related text in Times New Roman font (or your choice of font), referring to *Using a Computer to Generate Lettering* on pages 10–11 as necessary. The example above shows words and sayings printed in a variety of sizes and tones, ranging from light gray to black. When you have composed documents with the text and font of your choice, print out several copies. Antique the words as you did the images, using a sea sponge to apply the coffee solution. Leave some of the paper white. Allow the paper to dry completely.

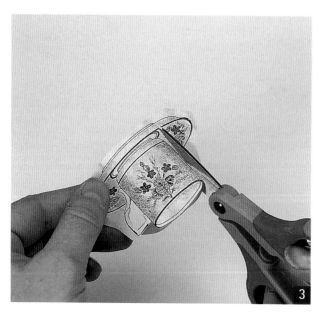

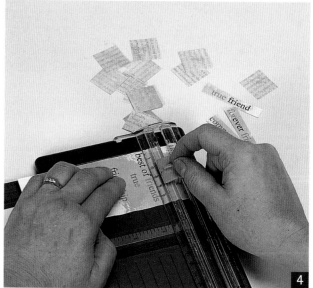

3 | Cut out images | Use a sharp craft knife to cut out any interior openings in the images, such as the space inside the teacup handle. With scissors, roughly cut out the image, allowing a ¼" (6mm) space around the perimeter. Holding the scissors at a 45° angle to the paper, move the paper, not the scissors, to cut precisely along the edges of the image.

4 | Cut out words | Use a sliding paper trimmer to cut each word into an individual strip. Cut decorative paper embellished with text into 1" (3cm) squares and other various rectangular sizes. (I used a piece of decorative paper, but you could easily replicate the look of the decorative paper by antiquing another computer-generated document.)

5 | Wax wooden backboard | Rub a stick of beeswax or the stub of a white candle along the wood surface wherever you would like it to look weathered, especially along the edges. The more wax you apply, the more worn and distressed the painted wood will look.

6 | Paint wood surface | Brush one coat of Trail Tan acrylic paint over the surface of the board. Allow the paint to dry, then apply another layer of wax in the same manner as before.

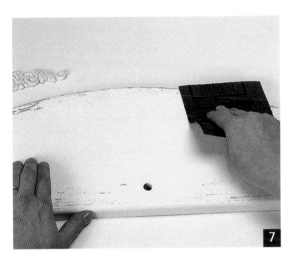

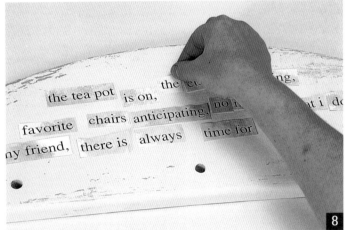

7 | Repaint and sand wood surface | Add one coat of Antique White acrylic paint, then allow the paint to dry. Using 100-grit sandpaper, sand the surface of the painted wood. During the sanding, the paint in the waxed areas will come off easily, resulting in a distressed appearance. Wax, paint and sand the carved wooden accent in the same manner.

8 | Découpage words | Découpage the words and decorative text onto the backboard, referring to the *Découpaging* guidelines on page 22 as necessary. Bounce the word strips a bit to give the text a more playful look. Burnish all the text, then give the backboard two coats of découpage medium to seal the elements, allowing the medium to dry between each coat.

9 | Wax and paint chairs | Wax each chair and corresponding wooden button along the edges and in any other areas you want to look weathered. Paint the chairs using Antique White, Cactus Green and Hydrangea Pink, making each chair different by painting the legs, seat and backrest different colors on all three. Allow the paint to dry, then sand the chairs to achieve the distressed look.

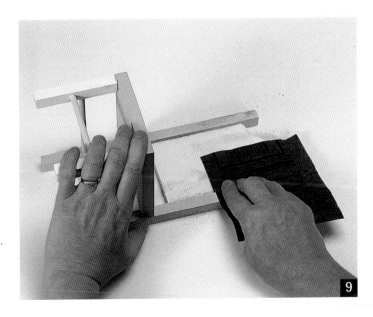

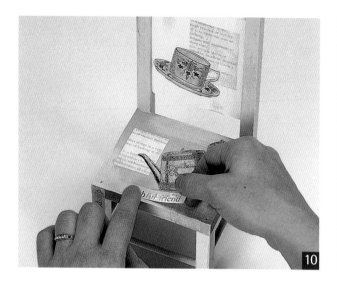 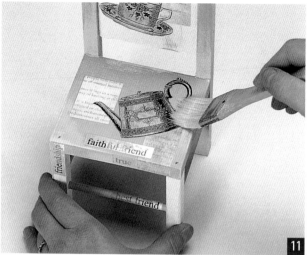

10 | Découpage each chair | Découpage each chair with decorative paper, images and words. Apply the decorative paper first, the images next and the words last. Burnish down all the paper elements, then give the chairs two coats of découpage medium to seal the elements, allowing the medium to dry between each coat.

11 | Apply satin varnish to chairs and board | After the découpage medium has dried completely, brush two coats of satin varnish onto the chairs and the backboard, allowing the varnish to dry between each coat. The varnish brings out the grain pattern on the exposed wood and gives the shelf a beautiful, hard finish.

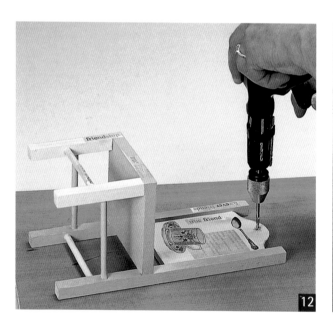 

12 | Drill holes in chairs | Determine the top center point of each chair backrest and mark the points with a pencil. Place the chair on another surface, such as a thick wooden board, to protect your tabletop while drilling. Use a hand drill to drill through the marked point on each chair.

13 | Secure chairs to backboard | Measure and mark the placement for each chair on the backboard. Use 1" (3cm)-long woodscrews to secure the chairs to the backboard. (Longer screws may go through the back of the board and scratch your wall once the shelf is mounted.) You can reinforce the screws with glue, but do not use glue as the only means of securing the chairs.

14 | Add buttons | With white glue, attach the decorative wooden buttons to conceal the screw holes. Use white glue and small finishing nails to attach the carved wooden accent to the top center of the backboard.

IN OTHER WORDS

Use your choice of words, phrases and sayings to embellish the *Tea Time Chair Shelf.* Looking for a little inspiration? Here are some ideas you may find helpful:

- My friend
- Forever friends
- Companionship
- Understanding
- Patient
- Best of friends
- True
- Friendship
- Faithful friend
- Loyal
- Trustworthy

The Finished Look

Hung in a kitchen nook, this special shelf promises to be an attention-getting conversation piece. It is functional as well; display items by placing them on the seats or hanging them from the chair rungs.

Variation: tea time clock

You'll know when it's "tea time" with this charming clock, made to match the Chair Shelf. Paint and découpage a square wooden plaque in a style similar to the shelf, then drill a hole through the middle and add the clock mechanism.

97

Sure to be a focal point in your home, this remarkable tiled tabletop is decorated with layers of fine-art images and text.

Tumbled marble tabletop

The Renaissance style has a timeless beauty, with its classical look inspired by ancient Rome. The Latin text used in this project was taken from a tablet that recorded Rome's glory with lapidary inscriptions. Other sources of Latin lapidary work include *Via Appia* monuments, the Arch of Constantine and the Trajan Column in Rome. Some other Latin expressions that you may find inspiring are listed on page 105.

TECHNIQUES USED IN THIS PROJECT
Using a Computer to Generate Lettering (pages 10–11)
Antiquing Paper (page 23)
Rubber Stamping (page 14)
Applying a Polymer Coating (pages 24–25)

MATERIALS AND TOOLS

12" x 12" (30cm x 30cm) craft plywood board or plaque, at least ⅜" (10mm) thick

two 6" (15 cm), two 4" (10 cm) and ten 2" (5 cm) square tumbled marble tiles

wooden moulding to fit around plywood board, plain or decorative

computer (with Caesar or other desired font) and printer

brushes
   basecoating brush
   soft, wide brushes
   disposable glue brushes

sponge

all-purpose acrylic sealer

matte acrylic spray, or extra-fine steel wool (000 or 0000) and carnauba car wax

rubber stamps with Renaissance-themed images, such as Leonardo's female head {THOUGHTFUL BY JUDIKINS}, Vitruvian Man {BY JUDIKINS}, castle icons {BY STAMPENDOUS, INC.} and decorative motifs {BY STAMPENDOUS, INC.}

dye ink pads
   metallic gold
   black

standard white computer paper

découpage paper with Renaissance-style images, such as Michelangelo's Sistine Chapel art {SISTINE CHAPEL BY ARTIFACTS, INC.}

Lazertran transfer decal paper

supplies for transferring decal paper
   small bowl of warm water
   turpentine
   pins

moulding cutter, or miter box and saw

hammer and small nails

antiquing solution, ¼ cup (60ml) instant coffee granules mixed with 2 cups (474ml) hot water

paper towels and waxed paper

thin white glue

scissors

clear tape

Envirotex Lite polymer coating

polymer coating supplies
   disposable plastic measuring cup
   small disposable plastic cups
   wooden stir sticks
   disposable glue brushes
   disposable latex gloves
   heat gun

notched trowel

tile adhesive, available at hardware stores or in mosaic section of craft stores

disposable, flexible, plastic container or pail

non-sanded grout

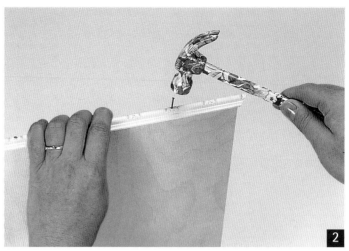

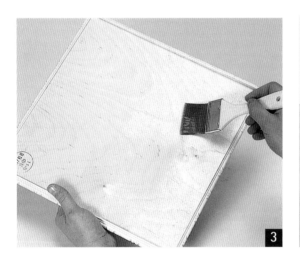

1 | **Cut moulding for tabletop** | Use a moulding cutter to cut four lengths of moulding to frame the 12" x 12" (30cm x 30cm) board. The cutter will trim the moulding at a 45° angle. If you do not have a molding cutter, use a miter box and saw to cut the moulding in the same manner.

2 | **Frame plywood** | Fit one length of moulding along the edge of the plywood, then secure it by hammering nails through the moulding into the wood. Repeat for all four sides until the plywood is framed.

3 | **Seal plywood** | Brush on one coat of acrylic sealer over the plywood and moulding.

4 | **Print and tear out text** | On a computer, lay out your chosen text in Caesar or another desired font, referring to the guidelines for *Using a Computer to Generate Lettering* on pages 10–11 as necessary. Vary the size and orientation of the lettering. To limit the text to the size of the tiles, type the words in text boxes measuring 6" x 6" (15cm x 15cm), 4" x 4" (10cm x 10cm) and 2" x 2" (5cm x 5cm). Frame each text box with a faint gray border to use as a guide when tearing out the text. Print several copies of the documents, then tear out each text box, staying within the border lines. Tear some of the text boxes in half or in thirds; this will simulate cracks in the marble. Tear out some blank pieces of paper as well.

5 | **Antique paper** | Use a soft, wide paintbrush and coffee solution to antique all of the torn paper pieces, using the *Antiquing Paper* technique described on page 23. With a paper towel, dab off excess solution in the center, but allow the solution to darken the edges. Allow the coffee solution to dry.

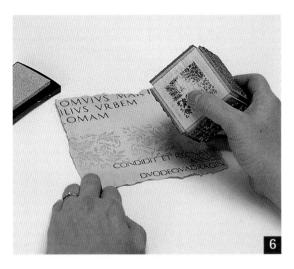

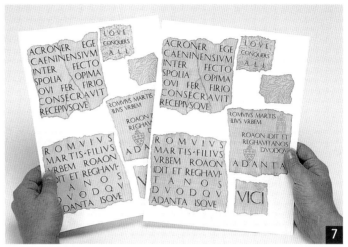

6 | **Stamp designs** | Stamp various designs onto the antiqued pieces of paper. Stamp some designs over the text, some between the text and some on the blank pieces. I used a metallic gold ink pad for a subtle effect against the coffee-stained paper.

7 | **Create master sheet** | Create a master sheet by gluing the torn, antiqued pieces of paper onto a sheet of white paper. If you ripped any text in half or in thirds, piece it back together as you glue it down. Also create a master sheet of images, including any pictures that you may want to use, such as art from the Sistine Chapel. Use a color copier to copy your master sheets onto sheets of Lazertran.

Note: Do not use a computer printer to print images onto Lazertran.

8 | **Cut out text and images** | Cut the images and text out of the Lazertran sheet, leaving a ⅛" (3mm) border of white around each design.

9 | **Prepare tile** | Lay out a sheet of waxed paper on your work surface. Fill a small bowl with warm water and place it nearby. Using a disposable glue brush, apply a single thin coat of turpentine onto a tile.

10 | **Soak transfer decal paper in water** | Select the Lazertran design elements you would like to place on the first tile. Place the first piece of Lazertran in the bowl of warm water and leave it in for about one minute, or until the paper curls up.

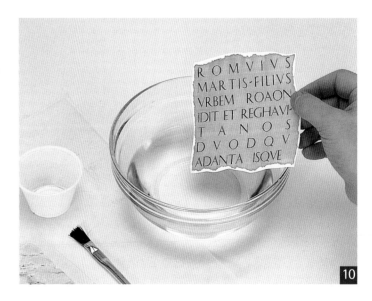

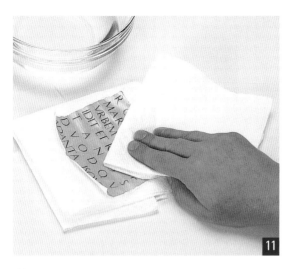

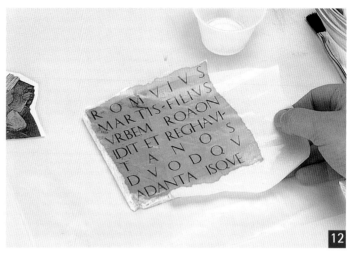

11 | **Remove transfer decal paper from water** | Take the Lazertran out of the water, uncurl it and place it on a folded paper towel. Dab the Lazertran with another folded paper towel to absorb excess water.

12 | **Remove bottom carrier sheet** | Place the wet Lazertran over the tile as desired. When the Lazertran is in position, slide the carrier sheet out from beneath so only the transparency is left on top of the tile. Adjust the transparency's position as necessary, then gently press down on it with a folded paper towel to remove any excess water.

13 | **Brush on more turpentine** | With the disposable glue brush, apply another thin layer of turpentine over the tile. If necessary, use the brush to fold the transparency over the edges of the tile. The turpentine will dissolve the Lazertran sheet and allow it to mold to the tile's irregular surface. For this reason, you should not try to adjust or move the Lazertran once you have applied the turpentine.

14 | **Add second layer of transfer decal paper** | If you want to overlay text and images, repeat the soaking process with a Lazertran image. Place the image directly on top of the text-covered tile, remove the carrier sheet and position as desired.

15 | **Apply another layer of turpentine** | Brush another thin coat of turpentine on top of the Lazertran and allow the turpentine to dry. If you see any bubbles, punch them out by lightly tapping your finger on them. If you find a stubborn bubble, use a pin to pop it. Repeat steps 9–15 to decorate all the tiles with Lazertran text and/or images.

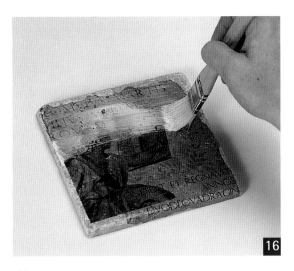

16 | **Apply two coats of glue** | When the turpentine is completely dry, brush a coat of thin white glue over all your tiles. As you apply the glue, it may bead. Allow the glue to dry clear, then add another coat. The glue should not bead on the second application. Allow the glue to dry completely.

17 | **Prepare for polymer coating** | Cover your work surface with several sheets of waxed paper. Turn each tile over and line the edges of the bottom surface with clear tape, as shown. Elevate the tiles faceup on small inverted plastic cups.

18 | **Coat tiles with polymer** | Follow the *Applying a Polymer Coating* instructions on pages 24–25 to finish each tile with a thick, waterproof polymer coating.

19 | **Cure and clean surface** | Let the tiles cure overnight. Once the tiles have cured, remove any drips that may have formed by pulling off the tape from the bottom of each tile.

20 | **Secure tiles to plywood** | Decide how you want to arrange the tiles on the framed plywood. Using a notched trowel, cover the plywood surface with tile adhesive. Press the tiles onto the plywood according to your arrangement, allowing no more than a 1/8" (3mm) space between the tiles.

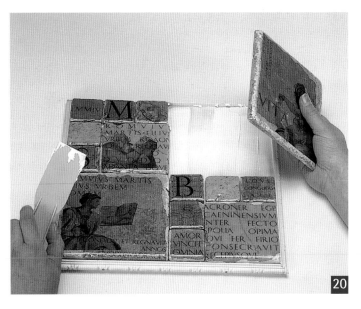

21 | **Mix grout** | Mix the grout in a disposable, plastic, flexible container. Pour dry grout into the container and gradually add cool water, stirring with a trowel until the consistency is stiff yet workable and not too soupy.

Note: To skip this mixing step, you can purchase premixed grout.

22 | **Apply grout** | Elevate the tiled plywood on several small inverted plastic cups. Use a trowel to apply the grout, working it into the grout lines between the tiles and around the edges of the tiles. Don't worry about getting grout on the frame or about scratching the surface of the tiles. When finished, smooth the grout by running your finger or a craft stick over all the grout lines. Allow the grout to sit for about ten minutes.

Note: Dispose of any unused grout by allowing it to harden in the container and then throwing it out in the trash bin. Never put grout down a drain.

23 | **Clean tiled surface** | Using a damp sponge, rub the surface of the tiles with warm water to remove the excess grout. Allow the surface to dry. Continue sponging the tiles until all the grout is removed and the surface no longer has a hazy film on it when dry. When the surface is clean, allow the grout to cure completely.

24 | **Coat frame with grout** | Mix another batch of grout in a small plastic cup, adding water to the grout to make a thick slurry. Using a disposable brush, coat the moulding with the grout mixture. Add as many coats as necessary to cover the wood. (If the moulding has a decorative design, the grout may fill in part of the design.) Allow the grout to cure completely.

25 | Finish tile surface | Spray the tabletop with matte acrylic finish. Or, to achieve a beautiful satin finish, rub the tiles with 000- or 0000-steel wool and a little water. Continue rubbing until you take off the shine, then finish the tiles by polishing them with carnauba wax.

IN OTHER WORDS

Use your choice of words, phrases and sayings to embellish the *Tumbled Marble Tabletop*. Looking for a little inspiration? Here are some ideas you may find helpful:

Proximo sed nolo fumigare. (Close but no cigar.)

Libens, volens, potens. (Ready, willing and able.)

Amor vincit omnia. (Love conquers all.)

Senilis et lardum...quom sophos. (Old and fat, but wise.)

Ars longa, vita brevis. (Art is long, but life is short.)

Non mihi, non tibi, sed nobis. (Not for me, not for you, but for us)

Die dulci fruere. (Have a nice day.)

The Finished Look

The size of this functional tiled tabletop can be increased by covering a larger plywood base with more tiles. Finish the project by securing the tabletop to a base. Wrought iron tables with 12" (30cm) tile tabletops are available in many craft and home decorating stores. Or, use the tiles to cover the top of an existing piece of furniture, such as a coffee table, for a new look.

Variation: coasters

While making the tabletop, decorate and coat extra tiles to use as coasters. After the polymer coating has cured, add cork buttons to the bottom of the tiles. A set of four coasters makes an impressive gift!

Standout spice box

This spice box gives "culinary art" a new meaning! In the project, the lettering serves two functions. First, it forms the names of your favorite, most-used spices, which feature prominently on the box lid. Second, the lettering acts as the main design element, used to embellish the decorative tiles covering the sides of the box. Matching spice tins accessorize the box, providing a unique touch to complete the set.

MATERIALS AND TOOLS

wooden box, 10¼" x 10¼" x 3½" (26cm x 26cm x 9cm), with 1½" (4cm) feet

nine 1¼" (3cm) square wooden tiles

gold knob for top handle

six watch tins with clear lids, 2¾" (7cm) diameter, 1" (3cm) deep

computer and printer

Delta Ceramcoat acrylic paint
- Lavender
- Nightfall Blue

acrylic spray sealer (not matte spray)

satin découpage medium

satin acrylic varnish

brushes
- brushes for basecoating and varnishing
- all-purpose natural bristle brushes
- fabric brushes
- disposable glue brush

rubber stamps
- freestanding typeface design {CHRISTMAS DEFINITIONS BY JUDIKINS}
- cursive script design {ITALIAN POETRY BACKGROUND BY HERO ARTS}
- letter alphabet set {ABC & 123 BY ALL NIGHT MEDIA/PLAID ENTERPRISES, INC.}
- paisley motif {BY PAPER PARACHUTE}

dye ink pads
- purple
- teal
- ultramarine

uppercase alphabet stencil {FANCY CAPS BY WORDSWORTH}

paper
- white card stock or sheets of 1" x 1" (3cm x 3cm) mosaic squares
- lilac card stock
- metallic gold card stock
- 12" x 12" (30cm x 30cm) sheets of dark green suede paper

100-grit sandpaper

sliding paper trimmer

metal ruler

disappearing ink pen (water-erase or air-erase pen), available from scrapbooking supply or fabric stores

paper towels

double-sided tape

waxed paper

mosaic motif paper punch {BY ALL NIGHT MEDIA/PLAID ENTERPRISES, INC.}

scissors

thin white glue

hand drill

wooden board

TECHNIQUES USED IN THIS PROJECT

Applying a Basecoat (page 20)
Rubber Stamping (page 14)
Stenciling (pages 16–18)
Using a Computer to Generate Lettering (pages 10–11)

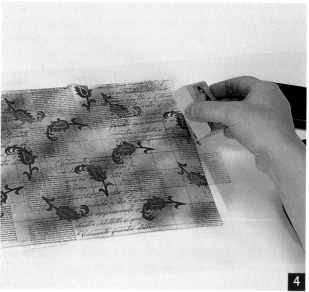

1 | **Basecoat box and lid** | Basecoat the exterior of the box, the edges, the inside of the lid, the round feet and the interior sides of the box with Nightfall Blue acrylic paint, sanding between each application, as directed in the *Applying a Basecoat* instructions on page 20. Apply a basecoat of Lavender acrylic paint to the top of the lid, sanding between each application.

2 | **Create decorative sheets** | Ink a dry, all-purpose natural bristle brush by pressing it into a purple ink pad. Make color drifts across a sheet of heavy paper, stippling and rubbing the ink in evenly spaced diagonal bands. I inked a sheet divided into self-adhesive 1" (3cm) mosaic squares, used for scrapbooking and stamping; however, you can use card stock and later cut it into 1" (3cm) squares. Using a separate brush for each color, repeat with teal ink and ultramarine ink until you have filled the page with color bands. Make a second sheet for the spice tins. (If you have only one brush, do not rinse it to remove the ink. Rather, remove the residual ink by rubbing the brush on a paper towel.)

3 | **Stamp decorative sheets** | Select two different stamps, one with a freestanding typeface and another with cursive script. Following the *Rubber Stamping* guidelines on page 14, stamp the paper. Ink the largest stamp with purple ink and stamp it on the paper three or four times in various places. Ink the other stamp in teal, then stamp it on the paper to fill in the remaining blank space. You can overlap the stamps and run the designs off the paper as desired.

4 | **Stamp paisley design** | Finish the design by stamping a paisley motif or some other heavier motif onto the paper with purple, teal and ultramarine ink, again overlapping the previously stamped pattern and running over the edge of the paper.

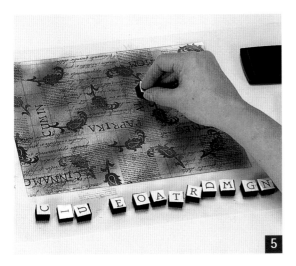

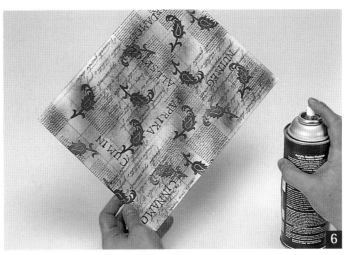

5 | Add words to paper | Using all three inks, add the names of different spices across the decorative sheets with either letter stamps or stencils. Orient the words in different directions, and don't worry about stamping or stenciling them in a perfectly straight line.

6 | Seal with acrylic spray | Spray each sheet with two coats of acrylic sealer (not matte spray), which will prevent the stamped ink from running in the following steps.

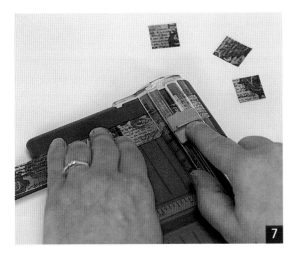

7 | Divide decorative sheet into squares | Divide the decorative sheets into 1" (3cm) square tiles. If you stamped on card stock, use a sliding paper trimmer to cut the square tiles apart. If you stamped on a sheet of self-adhesive mosaic squares, begin to pull the squares apart from the carrier sheet. Leave a few inches of the sheet uncut for use in step 24.

8 | Place tiles on box exterior | Arrange the tiles in rows along the exterior sides of the box, spacing them apart to form a faux grout line between each tile. You can arrange the tiles in the correct order to give a continuity of design, or you can arrange them in random order. Adhere the square tiles as placed, using découpage medium for card stock tiles or the sticky backing for self-adhesive tiles. Cover all four sides of the box with tiles. You should still have several tiles remaining for later use.

9 | Brush with satin varnish | Burnish the tiles until all are flush against the box surface. Brush two light coats of satin varnish over every basecoated surface of the box, including the tiled sides, letting the first coat dry before the second application.

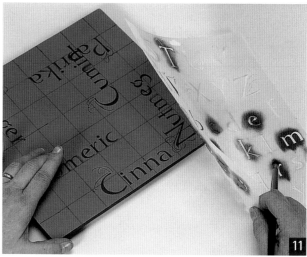

10 | **Create grid on box lid** | Using a metal ruler as a guide, lay out a grid on the top of the box lid with a disappearing-ink pen, spacing the lines 1½" (4cm) apart.

Note: The ink from disappearing-ink pens, also known as air-erase or water-erase pens, will disappear in the air or with water. In more humid areas, the erasable ink will tend to disappear faster.

11 | **Stencil words onto lid** | Pounce a fabric brush into the purple ink pad, then rouge the ink over the stencil to add names of spices along the grid lines. With another brush, use ultramarine ink to apply words in the same manner, overlapping the words to create depth and an interesting composition. (If you have only one brush, remove the residual purple ink by rubbing the brush on a paper towel, then ink it with the ultramarine.) Rotate the lid after each word to keep the composition balanced. You should have to add only seven to ten words to fill the space.

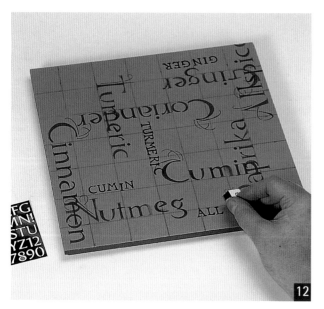

12 | **Stamp words onto lid** | Add more spice names to the lid in smaller letters using rubber stamps and teal ink. Fill empty spaces with words, following along the tops and bottoms of the grid lines.

13 | **Add decorative tiles to lid** | Again using the grid as your guide, fill in any remaining blank spots by adhering some of the remaining decorative tiles to the lid.

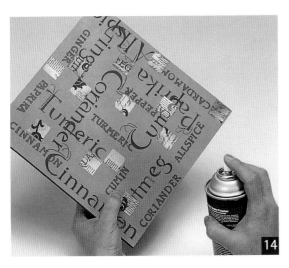

14 | **Seal with acrylic spray and satin finish** | Spray acrylic sealer over the top of the lid. This will prevent the ink from running when varnished. Once the sealer is dry, brush on two coats of satin varnish, allowing the first coat to dry before adding the second.

15 | **Paint wooden tiles** | Run a layer of double-sided tape over a piece of waxed paper, then attach the square wooden tiles to the tape. Brush two coats of lavender acrylic paint onto the tiles. Allow the paint to dry.

16 | **Create decorative accents** | Use the mosaic-motif paper punch to create designs on metallic gold card stock. Cut out each design within a square border to fit on top of the square wooden tiles, as shown. Brush découpage medium on the back of each accent, then adhere one to each tile.

17 | **Add wooden tiles to lid** | Position the wooden tiles on the lid as desired, then use thin white glue to attach them. Allow the glue to dry.

18 | **Drill center hole** | Glue one wooden tile precisely at the center of the lid exterior. Measure the center point of the lid, then hand drill a hole into the tile, penetrating all the way through the lid.

Note: To protect your work surface, be sure that there is a barrier under the lid, such as a thick wooden board, before drilling through it.

19 | **Attach handle** | Place the handle knob through the center hole and tighten to secure.

20 | **Line interior with suede** | Brush white glue onto the interior of the box bottom and box lid. Adhere one piece of suede paper, cut to size, to each surface.

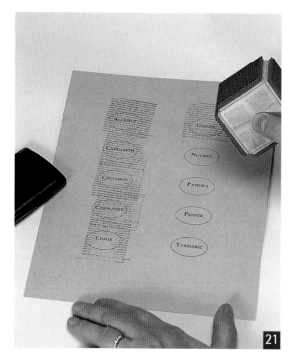

21 | **Print spice names** | Using a computer printer, print out the names of various spices in dark blue ink on lavender paper, with a purple oval around each word. Refer to *Using a Computer to Generate Lettering* on pages 10–11 as necessary. Ink a text stamp with ultramarine ink, then lightly stamp over each spice name to provide a background design.

22 | **Shade around oval** | Pounce a fabric brush into the purple ink pad, then add a light shade of purple around the oval border.

23 | **Label spice tins** | Cut out each oval label, leaving a small space around the oval border. Use double-sided tape to adhere the ovals to the lids of the watch tins.

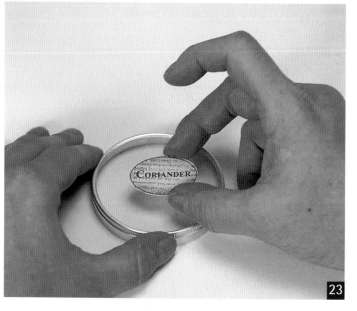

24 | Embellish spice tins | Cut several long strips of your decorative paper (or short strips from the mosaic squares) to fit around the sides of each spice tin. Wrap the paper strips around the tins, using double-sided tape to adhere them.

IN OTHER WORDS

Use your choice of words, phrases and sayings to embellish the *Standout Spice Box.* Looking for a little inspiration? Here are some ideas you may find helpful:

- Allspice
- Cardamom
- Cinnamon
- Coriander
- Cumin
- Ginger
- Nutmeg
- Paprika
- Turmeric

The Finished Look

This impressive lettered box makes a wonderful gift idea for a culinary-talented friend, although you may be tempted to keep it for yourself!

Variation: memory page

Sometimes a technique from one project inspires the creation of a completely different project. This memory page features different words, but the same lettering styles, handmade decorative paper tiles and ink colors as the spice box.

Don't let the prospect of sewing and hand lettering this decorative pillow intimidate you!

Friendship pillow

This beautiful pillow, lettered with the saying, *Friends are flowers that never fade*, is surprisingly easy to make. To create the elegant lettering, simply print out the saying on a computer—I chose the Edwardian Script font—or handwrite it on a piece of paper, if you prefer your own penmanship. Then, trace over the saying on the fabric surface with fabric paint. Attached to the pillow with needle and thread, the fabric panel is an easily removable and replaceable decoration. With an entire set of panels, you can change the look of the pillow on a whim.

MATERIALS AND TOOLS

15" (38cm) plain square pillow

computer (with Edwardian Script or other desired font) and printer

metallic gold dimensional fabric paint

standard white computer paper

light-colored (white or cream) 100% cotton fabric

decorative or patterned fabric, any material

T-shirt transfer paper for computer printers

postcard-size antique floral image, available on CD-ROM {SWEET ROSES BY THE VINTAGE WORKSHOP}

rotary cutter

self-healing cutting mat

metal ruler

scissors

iron and ironing board

low-tack masking tape

four white decorative buttons

pins

needle and thread (white or cream)

liquid fray preventer, available at fabric stores

TECHNIQUES USED IN THIS PROJECT

Using a Computer to Generate Lettering (pages 10–11)

Hand Lettering (page 12)

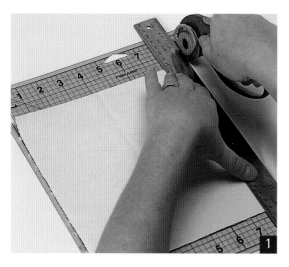

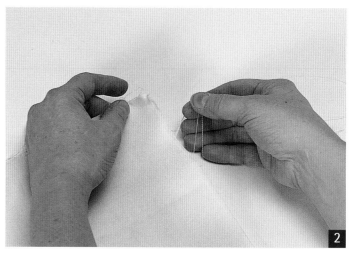

1 | **Cut fabric squares** | Cut the fabric squares with the rotary cutter, using a cutting mat and metal ruler. Cut the cotton fabric to a 9" (23cm) square and the other material to an 11½" (29cm) square.

2 | **Fray edges** | Fray about ⅛" (3mm) of the edges on both fabric squares by pulling the threads from each side. This adds a decorative touch but also ensures that the edges are straight and square.

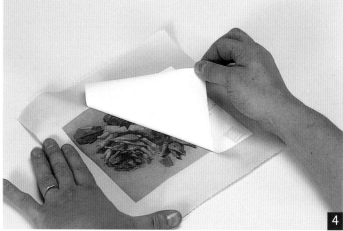

3 | **Print floral design** | Using a computer printer, print a vintage floral design onto T-shirt transfer paper. Cut out the design, leaving a ⅛" (3mm) border around the perimeter.

4 | **Iron design onto cotton square** | Turn an iron to the cotton setting (no steam), then place the transfer paper facedown on the cotton square with the image centered. On a hard surface, iron the transfer design onto the square, slowly moving the iron back and forth to avoid scorching any one area. Use your entire body to apply firm but even pressure with the iron. Let the transfer paper cool, then peel the backing paper off. If the backing paper doesn't come off, iron again. The transfer should leave a clean, crisp image.

5 | **Paint on lettering** | Using a computer, design and print the saying of your choice, with the exact size, font and spacing as it should appear on the pillow. This will serve as your text pattern. Place the pattern on a cutting mat, then align the cotton square on top. You should be able to see the text pattern beneath. Secure the pattern and the fabric square to the mat with low-tack masking tape. Starting from the upper-left corner (unless you're left-handed; then start at the opposite corner), trace over the lettering with fabric paint. As you work, outline the perimeter of the floral design with a series of dashes to simulate stitches. Use a small dab of the fabric paint to adhere a decorative button in each corner of the transfer design. Add two strokes of paint to form an *X* on the top of each button to simulate stitches holding the button.

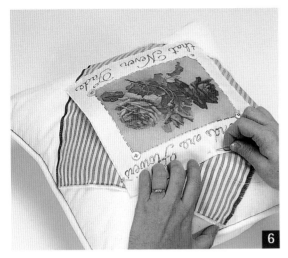

6 | **Finish edges and sew fabric squares to pillow** | After the gold paint has dried, turn the cotton square over. Apply a thin line of liquid fray preventer along the frayed edge. Apply the fray preventer to the back of the patterned fabric square as well. Let the fray preventer dry completely. Position the decorative fabric square on the pillow with the cotton square on top, as shown. Pin both in place at the corners. Use a needle to stitch the decorative fabric onto the pillow first, taking long stitches underneath the fabric and leaving small stitches on top. Sew on the cotton fabric with the same kind of stitch.

7 | **Paint over stitches** | With the fabric paint, cover each stitch on both fabric squares. Work on one side at a time, finishing all stitches on one side before moving to the next side.

The Finished Look

This friendship pillow makes a beautiful accent piece in a romantic or Victorian-inspired décor. Sayings on pillows are currently very popular. When combined with a vintage image, a saying or quote will make your pillow stand out in any room.

Variation: signed tablecloth

To commemorate an important event such as an anniversary, make and attach a decorative panel to a small, round tablecloth. Have friends and family sign the tablecloth with a water-erase pen, then trace the signatures with fabric paint; work promptly, as moisture in the air will eventually cause the water-erase marks to disappear.

Templates

On the following pages, you'll find the alphabet guides and templates used for the projects in this book. Use a photocopier to enlarge the templates as directed.

SMILE! WORD TEMPLATES

These words are for the *Smile! Silver Frame* on pages 28–33. There is no need to enlarge the words before transferring them to your surface.

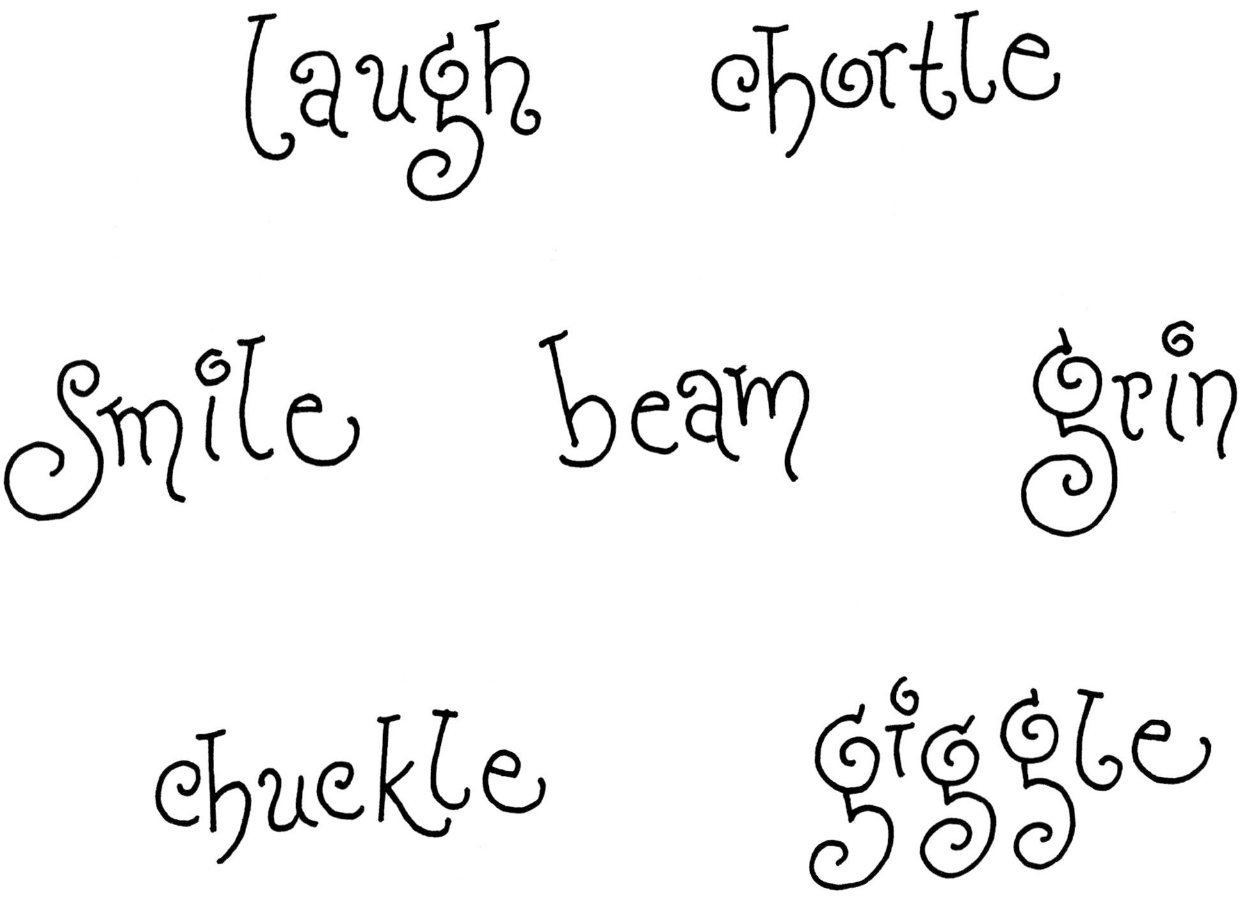

laugh   chortle

Smile   beam   grin

chuckle   giggle

CELTIC ALPHABET GUIDE

This alphabet guide is for the *Celtic Lettered Flowerpots* on pages 34–39. Each letter includes numbers and arrows to guide you through the strokes. If desired, enlarge the alphabets to the size you'll be using for the flowerpots.

BREAD BASKET DESIGN TEMPLATE

This pattern is for the *Italian Bread Basket Tray* on pages 72–77. Enlarge the pattern
153% before transferring it to your surface.

CASUAL ITALIAN ALPHABET GUIDE

This alphabet guide is for the *Italian Bread Basket Tray* on pages 72–77. You can use it to create any saying or expression. Enlarge the guide 182% before transferring the letters to your surface.

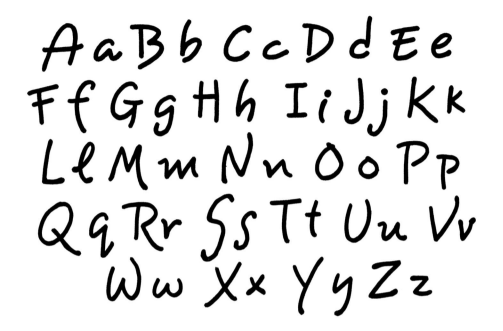

MOON AND STARS TEMPLATE

This pattern is for the *Baby Memory Box* on pages 78–83. Enlarge the pattern 167% before transferring it to your surface.

BLOCK LETTER ALPHABET TEMPLATE

This alphabet guide is for the *Baby Memory Box* on pages 78–83, to be used when making your own stencils. Enlarge the guide 146% before transferring the letters to your stencil surface.

Resources

I always recommend supporting local craft supply shops and hardware stores whenever possible, but not every store can carry everything. I have provided the manufacturer's information for the products used in this book so you can find distributors near you. The Web sites contain technical product support and useful information as well.

ADHESIVES

Beacon Adhesives
125 S. MacQuesten Parkway, Mt. Vernon, NY 10550
(914) 699-3400
www.beaconadhesives.com
general craft glues

Duncan Enterprises
5673 E. Shields Avenue, Fresno, CA 93727
(800) 438-6226
www.duncan-enterprises.com
general craft glues (including Stop Fray glue)

DECORATIVE PAPERS AND STICKERS

Artifacts, Inc.
P.O. Box 3399, Palestine, TX 75802
(800) 678-4178
www.artifactsinc.com
découpage paper (including Michelangelo's Sistine Chapel art)

Hot Off the Press, Inc.
1250 NW Third, Canby, OR 97013
(888) 300-3406
www.craftpizazz.com
découpage and decorative paper

K&Company
8500 NW River Park Drive, Parkville, MO 64152
(888) 244-2083
www.kandcompany.com
stickers (including English floral alphabet, English flower images, vines, borders, corners and journal tags), dimensional resin stickers (including Life's Journey domed Goudy alphabet), decorative paper (including English florals, English floral accents and Life's Journey letters), suede paper

Magenta
2275 Bombardier, Sainte-Julie, Quebec, Canada J3E 2J9
(450) 922-5253
www.magentastyle.com
decorative paper (including mosaic squares paper)

EMBELLISHMENTS

JewelCraft LLC
505 Winsor Drive, Secaucus, NJ 07094
(201) 223-0804
www.jewelcraft.biz
miniature square accent mirrors

Lee Valley Tools
P.O. Box 1780, Ogdensburg, NY 13669
USA: (800) 267-8735
CAN: (800) 267-8761
www.leevalley.com
watch tins

Making Memories
1168 W. 500 N., Centerville, UT 84014
(801) 294-0430
www.makingmemories.com
laser-cut metal words, Page Pebbles

Uchida of America, Corp.
3535 Del Amo Boulevard, Torrance, CA 90503
(800) 541-5877
www.uchida.com
erasable fabric markers

GILDING SUPPLIES

American Art Clay Co., Inc.
6060 Guion Road, Indianapolis, IN 46254
(800) 374-1600
www.amaco.com
Rub 'n Buff metallic paste

Jacquard Products/Rubert Gibbon & Spider, Inc.
P.O. Box 425, Healdsburg, CA 95448
(800) 442-0455
www.jacquardproducts.com
Pearl-Ex metallic powdered pigments

PAINTS, PAINTING SUPPLIES AND STENCILS

Delta
2550 Pellissier Place, Whittier, CA 90601
(800) 423-4135
www.deltacrafts.com
acrylic paints, acrylic mediums, acrylic varnishes and all-purpose sealers, texture paints, découpage medium, acrylic enamel paints and surface conditioners (PermEnamel), stencils (including Strokework vine border and Harlequin diamond background), stencil sponges

Hunt Corp.
2005 Market Street, Philadelphia, PA 19103
(215) 656-0300
www.hunt-corp.com
Painters metallic paint pens

Krylon
101 Prospect Avenue, NW, Cleveland, OH 44115
(800) 832-2541
www.krylon.com
sealer sprays (Clear Sealer), varnish sprays

Loew-Cornell, Inc.
563 Chestnut Avenue, Teaneck, NJ 07666
(201) 836-7070
www.loew-cornell.com
general painting supplies, paintbrushes and sea sponges, palette knives, Brush-Up paper, water-erasable transfer paper (Chacopaper)

Plaid Enterprises, Inc.
3225 Westech Drive, Norcross, GA 30092
(800) 842-4197
www.plaidonline.com
découpage paper (including Gorgeous Grapes), découpage medium, stencils (including Monogram Alphabet, small diamond border and 1" Upper Case Letters), dimensional fabric paint

Provo Craft
151 E. 3450 N., Spanish Fork, UT 84660
(800) 937-7686
www.provocraft.com
stencils, stickers (including Alphabiggies)

Wordsworth
3725 Cottage Drive, Colorado Springs, CO 80920
(719) 282-3495
www.wordsworthstamps.com
stencils (including Fancy Caps)

POLYMER CLAY

Kato Polyclay by Van Aken
P.O. Box 1680, Rancho Cucamonga, CA 91729
(909) 980-2001
www.katopolyclay.com
polymer clay, polymer clay tools

Polyform Products Co.
1901 Estes Avenue, Elk Grove Village, IL 60007
(847) 427-0020
www.sculpey.com
polymer clay supplies (including Stamplets templates)

POLYMER COATING

Environmental Technology Inc.
300 South Bay Depot Road, Fields Landing, CA 95537
(707) 443-9323
www.eti-usa.com
Envirotex Lite polymer coating, Ultra Seal (thin white glue for sealing), measuring cups, wooden stir sticks, disposable glue brushes

RUBBER STAMPS AND RUBBER STAMPING SUPPLIES

All Night Media
(see information for Plaid Enterprises, Inc.)
stamps (including ABC & 123 set), stamping supplies, paper punches (including mosaic motif)

Hero Arts
1343 Powell Street, Emeryville, CA 94608
(800) 822-4376
www.heroarts.com
stamps (including Vintage Alphabet, Whimsical Alphabet, Quatros swirl pattern and Italian Poetry Background), stamping supplies

JudiKins
17803 S. Harvard Boulevard, Gardena, CA 90248
(310) 515-1115
www.judikins.com
stamps (including Thoughtful, Vitruvian Man and Christmas Definitions), stamping supplies

PSX
5673 E. Shields Avenue, Fresno, CA 93727
(800) 438-6226
www.psxdesign.com
stamps (including lowercase and uppercase alphabet), stamping supplies

Paper Parachute
P.O. Box 91385, Portland, OR 97291
(503) 533-4513
www.paperchute.com
stamps (including paisley motif), stamping supplies

Stampendous, Inc.
1240 N. Red Gum, Anaheim, CA 92806
(800) 869-0474
www.stampendous.com
stamps (including castle icons and Foliate QuadCube), stamping supplies

Tsukineko
17640 NE Sixty-fifth Street, Redmond, WA 98002
(425) 883-7733
www.tsukineko.com
stamping supplies (including Staz-On ink stamp pads and cleaner)

USArtQuest
7800 Ann Arbor Road, Grass Lake, MI 49240
(517) 522-6225
www.usartquest.com
stamps, rubber lettering plates (Calligraphic Background Prints), stamping supplies

TOOLS

Fiskars Brands, Inc.
7811 W. Stewart Avenue, Wausau, WI 54401
(800) 500-4849
www.fiskars.com
scissors, decorative-edged scissors, embossing pads and styluses, plastic shape templates, hand drills, sliding paper trimmers, craft knives, self-healing cutting mats, rotary cutters

TRANSFERS, TRANSFER SUPPLIES AND COPYRIGHT-FREE IMAGES

Dover Publications
31 E. Second Street, Mineola, NY 11501
(516) 294-7000
www.doverpublications.com
copyright-free clip art (including Old Time Label Art wine labels)

Lazertran LLC
650 Eighth Avenue, New Hyde Park, NY 11040
(800) 245-7547
www.lazertran.com
transfer decal paper

The Vintage Workshop
P.O. Box 30237, Kansas City, MO 64112
(913) 648-2700
www.thevintageworkshop.com
antique images on CD-ROM (including Sweet Roses)

WOODEN SURFACES

Midwest Products Co., Inc.
400 S. Indiana Street, Hobart, IN 46342
(800) 348-3497
www.midwestproducts.com
craft plywood, cutter (Easy Cutter) for moulding

Stone Bridge Collection
(613) 624-5080
www.stonebridgecollection.com
wooden products: trays, basket trays (Charing Cross), oval bentwood boxes, frames (including octagon frames)

Walnut Hollow Farm, Inc.
1409 State Road 23, Dodgeville, WI 53533
(800) 950-5101
www.walnuthollow.com
wooden products: frames, boxes, plaques, letters, accents, tiles, miniature chairs, pegboards

Index

Learn to make stunning crafts with these other fine North Light Books!

Gifts from the Heart
ISBN 1-58180-576-4, paperback, 96 pages, #33039-K

When only a handmade gift will do, turn to *Gifts from the Heart*. Inside, you'll find 60 gift-ideas you can make in an hour (many in just a few minutes) that will be cherished for a lifetime! From a fanciful nightlight and a bouquet of blooming pens to elegant notecard sets and spa gifts, these projects are fun to make, easy to personalize and pure joy to give.

Collage Creations
ISBN 1-58180-546-2, paperback, 128 pages, #32894-K

Fill your home with gorgeous, functional works of art! You'll discover over 20 step-by-step creative collage techniques to decorate home décor items and gifts using a range of creative materials from handmade paper and collage ephemera to rubber stamps, paint and other embellishments. You'll learn easy-to-master techniques for creating interesting backgrounds, giving paper an aged look, transferring images and more.

Classic Paper Techniques for Greeting Cards & Gifts
ISBN 1-58180-511-X, paperback, 128 pages, #32871-K

Some things just never go out of style—like the 10 timeless paper techniques for creating beautiful cards and gifts. Each step is fully illustrated so that learning is easy. In addition, Alisa Harkless shows you how to incorporate the techniques into 25 stunning step-by-step projects—everything from greeting cards to gift boxes and framed pieces of art.

Elegant Lettering for Your Home
ISBN 1-58180-578-0, paperback, 128 pages, #33041-K

Hand-painted lettering is a hot trend in home décor—and it's one that's here to stay. Whether it's a few words on an end table, etched lettering on glass kitchen canisters or a favorite quote transformed into a stunning wall border, stylish lettering enhances any room. In *Elegant Lettering for Your Home*, decorative artist Rebecca Baer provides you with everything you need for beautiful lettering designs.

NORTH LIGHT BOOKS

These and other fine North Light books are available at your local art & craft retailer, bookstore, online supplier or by calling 1-800-448-0915.

When calling please use promotion code TBA05NLB.